TONY SERRA

*The Green, Yellow and Purple Years
in the Life of a Radical Lawyer*

TONY SERRA

*The Green, Yellow and Purple Years
in the Life of a Radical Lawyer*

J. Tony Serra

Grizzly Peak Press
Kensington ~ CA

For information contact:
Grizzly Peak Press
350 Berkeley Park Blvd.
Kensington, CA 94707
www.grizzlypeakpress.com

Tony Serra
is published by Daniel N. David
and is distributed by
Grizzly Peak Press.

Design, layout and typesetting by
Liquid Pictures
www.liquidpictures.com

ISBN Number: 978-0-9839264-4-3
Library of Congress Number: 2014931316

Printed in the United States of America

Foreword

~

Forgive my romanticized and self-indulgent propositions in the forthcoming pages. Recall that such were written at Lompoc Federal Prison camp during my incarceration for U. S. Tax Resistance. I was not purporting to document case histories. You can find those references on the internet. Mine is not a quest for accuracy. Mine is a flight into whimsey and caprice, a retrospective twinkle in the eyes of memory: In short, confinement escapism.

I originally entitled the work as "The Green, Yellow and Purple Years in the Life of a Radical Lawyer." I originally categorized the manuscript as a "chromatic, metaphoric, autobiography of J. Tony Serra's defense of Black Panthers, the S. L. A., the New World Liberation Front, Nuestra Familia, Earth First, Hells Angels, Mafia and Native Americans, intertwined with his his anti-establishment ideology, written while in Federal Prison for tax resistance."

I wrote to sprinkle psychedelic remnants from my life in the sixties over sometimes a bleak and sorrowful state of mind; sort of an upheaval in prison camp as psychic relief. What I wrote was embroidered, embellished, grandiose, and self-serving. It suffers from myopic blindness, but is truly an eye peering intently on the melodramas in the theater of jury trial performance.

Not all of the book, however, is self-ebullience. It is not all sheen without solidarity. Accounts of my cases and political philosophy are real. I employed color metaphors, because color is the gateway to esthetic truth, and esthetic truths are parts of the foundations for social growth. My intended pursuit was polemic, to advance always the validity of the anti-thesis and nourish the anti-establishment.

J. Tony Serra, San Francisco, 2014

Table of Contents

~

Introduction

~

When I first arrived in San Francisco in the summer of 1966, I was amazed to find that all the dreams my fledgling generation sought were blossoming in a small area of the city around Golden Gate Park called the Haight-Ashbury.

I had just spent the last year learning about the military-industrial complex, aghast at the idea of corporations making money by creating misery. The Viet Nam War was in full swing, and we watched the defoliation, napalm, and body bags on nightly television.

Before arriving in the City, I had joined a liberal political group at LSU bent on ending the Vietnam War, stamping out voter discrimination based on race, and publicizing the activities of a certain Southern despot who had developed concentration camps for civil rights workers. Braced by the brave nuns and priests of the on-campus

Newman Club, I steeled my barely eighteen-year-old courage and joined the picket lines, in spite of the rhetoric of jeering, hostile crew-cut men.

In the Haight-Ashbury I found a larger group of young people from every part of the world, the migrations to San Francisco culminating in the Summer of Love, 1967. Each of the men and women on the street shared in a brotherhood, regardless of race, age, nationality, or religion, believing racism, poverty, unequal education, and war could be ended. We began to have our first inklings of the big movement that required protection of the planet, realizing our generation's stewardship of the earth. We started eating vegetables over meat, organic food instead of produce sprayed with poisons, balancing the body with yoga and meditation.

On Haight Street and in the Park, the Grateful Dead set up speakers and played music for free. Tickets to the Fillmore Auditorium were $2.50, and it was easy to stand next to the stage with a few hundred people to listen to Janis Joplin, Jim Morrison, David Crosby, and Grace Slick.

J. Tony Serra

Brotherhood was shared by the passing of the peace pipe and cemented by the sacramental use of LSD. The renaissance of the Sixties exploded in new art, music, light shows, political and social movements, organic food stores, and psychedelic chemists.

Enter the Blue Meanies.

Coming out of the ecstasy of days of sun and sharing in Golden Gate Park, we had to face the fact that there were those who could not tolerate freedom of speech, free thought, non-material goals, or communal living. Although the tour buses rolled up Haight Street, so did the occasional police street sweep, huge men with padded blue jackets, thick leather belts hanging with tear gas, wearing helmets, and carrying nightsticks and guns. While peace-loving hippies plotted ways to change the world to one of sensitivity and unity, kids were rounded up and arrested for possession or sales of sacraments important to the psychedelic revolution.

For the first time I heard the name Tony Serra. Tony was an attorney who wouldn't rip you off or leave you without counsel because you couldn't pay more on a lengthening case, someone who brilliantly knew the rules of the legal game and also understood that the fight was a battle—the people of vision pitted against those who would destroy the world in their lack of vision.

Almost fifty years later, Tony Serra's story has not changed. His book is more than an account of his fight against the drug laws and the young people he kept from jail in the Sixties, but about his commitment to the Constitution, the legal system he believes in and loves, and the men and women who have had the courage to work with him.

Tony Serra is the story of Tony's belief that government concerns people who give their consent to be governed, not manipulated and bullied by those who would make rules for their own gain at the expense of individuals and the environment.

It is a story of the abolition of class, and his knowledge that his life and work is to honor the living spark in every man, regardless of race or social status.

J. Tony Serra

Most importantly, it is the story of the fight against the encroachment of government to overstep and take away the guarantees of a free society.

From his defense of Huey Newton, charismatic leader of The Black Panthers, to Jacque Rogier of the New World Liberation Front, Russell Little of the Symbionise Liberation Army, to Patrick 'Hooty" Croy, Northern California Indian, Tony personifies the meaning of true courage, the amalgam of defendant and attorney feeding the other with the energy and brilliance to win.

The words of these pages are beautiful, as much poetry as prose. His story is wrapped around the colors of the rainbow, the language visceral, words exploding against the skin, slipping into the air to be breathed, images to be drunk. A magician, a shaman, a holy man, at moments I had to stop to catch my breath at the poignancy of his observations, the melding of many worlds of consciousness all coming together in one place. The language, the circumstances of the trials, his awareness of the actual battles underlying the courtroom, washes against the reader, giant waves of intellectual realization and emotion, forcing one to stop, to wonder, to question.

This book is a legacy, not only for those of us who read his words today, but for those generations to come who will have to face the power, lack of compassion, and simple-mindedness of an encroaching police state. These stories highlight the struggle between those who have and those who have not, the power of injustice fostered on the weak and poor by the police, the courts, and the Congress who voted for mandatory minimums, paid for with tax dollars squeezed from the very people who are rendered powerless by the system.

If the spirit ever falters, this book will be a classic touchstone of beauty, encouragement, and reason.

Pamela Johnson
A Nation of Mystics

This book is dedicated to the
Rainbows in the Courtroom.

TONY SERRA

The Green, Yellow and Purple Years
in the Life of a Radical Lawyer

The Green Years

~

I was born emerald green. I guess that I am one in a million in this respect. My mother told me that I glowed green iridescence in the dark as a baby and seemed to project a green halo. She said I was like a green jewel sparkling green rainbows from my crib. I was beautiful but eerie and mysterious to them. My parents tried to keep my greenness secret. They thought it would disappear as I grew, that it was just an infant phase. But I remained green for thirty years. I still sometimes shimmer with iridescence.

My greenhood enlarged as my childhood proceeded. A Kelly green moss covered my body; my hair was grass-like; my eyes like green hummingbird feathers. At times my arms and legs extended from my body as vines and tendrils. When I laughed, small green flowers floated out of my mouth. I would lie stomach down in the unkempt grasses of our backyard for hours staring sideways at the growing foliage in awe of its green strength. Green grass and green leaves, green snails and green bugs were my early fascination. When the wintergreen grasses first appeared, thin, and juicy, I would pluck handfuls and stuff it into my mouth. Eating young grass shoots was my favorite food.

I was raised in San Francisco, but from early teenage, I cavorted in West Marin an hour up the coast from the Golden Gate Bridge. Grassy rolling hills, spear-like reeds surrounding marshy wetlands, eucalyptus groves following brooks and streams to the sea and verdant pastures with waist high green tufted grass stalks waving in the wind: all formed the sculpture of the area. I visited upon it all with an intuitive vegetable unity. I was young, strong, erect like an immature fava bean. Green uncombed hair like carrot tops spilled over my head. My emerald eyes emitted green fire; my moss covered body glistened like turquoise. I ran wildly amongst the high grasses; I savored the eucalyptus leaves; I ate the fresh green nasturtium leaves, licking green pearls of dew from their centers. I was naked; I was a green growth pushing toward the sun; I was live jade in the greenness of early existence. The vital force of life pushing upward from the earth filled me and suffused my being. I became intelligent with vegetable, plant, tree and grass wisdom.

My path through college and law school was strewn with greenery. My feet never touched the earth. The grassy knolls and mounds surrounding Stanford University nourished my body and mind. Stanford's lush, manicured golf course lawns became my holy spot. The oak trees rained green leaves upon me; green snakes, green dragon flies, green frogs and toads, green lizards, green birds inspired truth, beauty and poetry within me. At night I smoked green-bud marijuana. I became a green Sprite and the Green Muses serenaded me by wind songs through green leafed trees, by dancing green grasses on the hills, by green moon faces on wet lawns. The entire greenness of earth nurtured me. Sports, studies, student comraderie, work, play and profound long leafy thoughts became my mental domain. Everyone seemed to rejoice in my greenness. They invited me to put it on display. The student environment saw its beauty and its strength. It spilled over onto them. I gave full reign to my rising greenhood. There was no question; there was no struggle. It was a gift; it was a grace. I was a green young man among supportative young men and women.

My life became performance. I became living poetry. I dressed in green silk. I danced and recited green poetry for them all. I shined and glittered green jewels. I rolled and reflected like a green sea. My early maturation was fecund: I bore green fruit: green peach, green corn; I harvested green lettuce, green tomato, green onion. Green frog, green finch, green flies surrounded me. To all people I gave a gift of greenness.

I graduated from University of California, Boalt Law School at Berkeley, California. The Haight Ashbury hippy sub-culture was burgeoning. Youth from all over the world traversed the streets of San Francisco. I saw other green people for the first time. I was overwhelmed. I took LSD with them. We became a unit, a moving green forest of tall trees. We were free. We were bold. We interwove our greenness; we made love with our green bodies and green minds. I became conscious that we the greens; we with the green auras; we with the vegetable strength of the live planet; we had a mission; we had a cause. My green buds were ready to blossom; I had green flowers to bestow on humankind. This became the creed of the green and greenish youth of the hippie era.

The green force must be harnessed. We, the green hippies, locked our branches, commingled our grasses and our organic growth, moss upon moss, leaf upon leaf; with all greenness conjoined, we would present ourselves as selfless servants to the betterment of the human condition. We would give ourselves to those who were black or brown or who hurt or were weak. That was our calling. We separated and went into the chaos of the real world, carrying high our green banner of excelsior.

I became a radical criminal trial lawyer. The Vietnam War was occurring. Protests and demonstrations were rampant. Political activism was reborn. Change and reform of law, of inequality, of social status, of economic opportunity, of education was on the move. I cast my greenness into it with all the vigor and intensity of my being.

I offered my first green bud of politics to the Black Panthers. It was the mid-70's. The Panther Movement was burgeoning across the country. I volunteered to sleep in their party headquarters in Oakland and San Francisco. We expected a police attack. I, as a lawyer, would be the potential mediator, or an objective witness, or even a victim. I slept in a sleeping bag near the front door. We were armed and sandbagged for protection. No police assault ever materialized, but I became trusted; I met Huey Newton when he returned from Cuba. The Panthers saw that I radiated greenness. It was unsaid but acknowledged that I was shamrock green clover in their midst.

Huey Newton, the servant to his people, the Party Chairman, the greatest charismatic human being that I have ever touched, cast his holy water upon me and incanted my fructifying growth. I was young and green, growing straight upward, tall, developing branches and leaves. My roots were spreading, absorbing. My broccolied brain was expanding. Under the horticultural expertise of Huey Newton, green buds appeared and burst out, firm and healthy throughout my limbs. The budding flowers of social justice. Racial equality and resistance to unfair police practices adorned my body. I chanted with the Black Panthers. I marched with them. I imbibed their words, heralded their deeds, fought their causes in Oakland, Berkeley and Martinez courts; my nurture was their successes. I was stalwart like a green ear of corn.

My first big case was Huey Newton's murder trial. It was alleged that he had killed a street prostitute. The prosecution was a sham and politically motivated. At least a dozen different and many mutually exclusive descriptions of the real assailant had been given. The major witness who had precipitated the arrest and prosecution of this national hero of Black People, who said she definitely eye-witnessed him kill the victim, turned out to have been in jail on the date of the occurrence. We easily prevailed, but only after a long and dramatic jury trial in downtown Oakland, California.

Huey was magnificent during the trial. His Black power smothered the opposition. His bare chested speeches on the stairs of the courthouse inspired cheering multitudes of supporters. "Power to the People," "Power to the People" became the mantra of the times. Every day of the trial, the courtroom was filled; the halls of the court floor were filled; the courthouse itself was surrounded by his sometimes riotous, sometimes solemn well-wishers; black and white, man and woman, child and adult rallied to the cause. Everyone knew that the prosecution was flawed by an ulterior motive to destroy the leadership of the movement.

Huey shared a small patch of this grandiose stage with me. He believed in youthful idealism; he was not a reverse racist. He allowed all races a portion of the revolutionary process. Power to the People meant power to all oppressed people. I knew that he wanted me there, at his side, at times, because of my greenness, my scintillating emerald color, my vegetable thrusting strength. Black power with rays of green light permeated the political dimension of the trial.

I remember being in the courtroom: an old varnished, wooden altar in an obsolete decadent cathedral, the thick audience heaving breath and heart beat in one unified rhythm. It wasn't a court of law; it was a church of law. We stood; the audience kneeled; we shouted; the audience murmured and nodded. I gave a five hour closing argument; the audience joined with me spontaneously: "You tell 'em, Tony"; "That's the way it is"; "Right on, Tony"; "Free Huey, Free Huey." I was a burning green light that day; they were hot green electricity. Huey was a font of green radiation. We were overwhelming. We were victorious.

At the end, a thousand green psychedelic, iridescent flies, almost blinding, massed over and covered the prosecutor. He was devoured by our greenness. We left triumphantly walking over an oil slick of green residue deposited permanently on the courtroom floor. Green papers on green front pages of newspapers gave glittering green accounts of our conquest, of our cause, of our ideology. On that single spectacular day, the Black Panthers turned the history of Black peoples' struggle for equality in this country into a rising green dragon on the horizon.

Green had dominated the trial. It had infiltrated darkness. We had sent green radiance into the black hole of the judge's bench. We had ensnared the prosecution with vines. I had stood in the court on mowed and unmowed grass. I had sermoned on green worms and birds: green fish had swum out of my mouth. I glowed; fluttered, swirled about them. All colors of green, green prismatic rainbows, shades of greenness engulfed the courtroom, infused the jury. Grass grew in the halls of the Hall of Justice. My thoughts, my words, my ideas gushed greenly from my throat. It was a rush, an unstoppable force - a core of life thrust - an energy of the green sea, the green earth, the green planet. Huey Newton's trial for me was my first experience in harnessing the green force that underlies all life on earth.

J. Tony Serra

That night we celebrated in a green swirl of ecstacy - we ate green cake, green cheese, drank green liquor - we sated on green; we thought green; we danced green. VIRID, VERDURE, VIRIDESENCE ruled the Black of the Panthers and the green of their lawyer and turned the night reflective cobalt green.

·The Huey Newton victory established me as a premier radical criminal trial lawyer. I would never be in need thereafter of fame or fortune. It humbled me greatly. In an LSD session, I took a vow of poverty. I pledged never to capitalize on the practice of law. I adopted the Marxian theorem of from each according to his ability; to each according to his need. I denounced capitalism, private ownership of property and major business. I rejected probate laws that allow one generation to pass accumulated wealth to another generation. I rejected corporations that allow unlimited expansion and profit and interfere with the workings of democracy. I resisted thereafter taxation which falls dominantly on the consumer and wage earners, the true tax victims. In essence, I adopted everything that I believed was philosophically helpful in dedicating my life to the selfless service of its people. I still thank Huey Newton for this ideological gift.

To this date (2006), I haven't made profit from law. I own nothing but old clothes and artifacts; I have no real property, no money in the bank, no stocks, no trusts. I live from hand to mouth. Everything I make beyond my expenses I put into my pro bono cases. There is never a surplus. As I write this from Lompoc Federal Prison Camp, having been sentenced to prison for ten months for willful failure to pay federal income tax, I am penniless. I have diligently practiced criminal defense law for forty-three years. This is my second time in federal prison camp. I have suffered three misdemeanor convictions for tax over the years, none of which were moral turpitude crimes. My license to practice has never been revoked.

After the Huey Newton trial, I entered into a jungle period of legal practice. I tried jury case after case. I was inexhaustible. I was like a sinuous line of fast growing green bamboo shoots.

J. Tony Serra

I infiltrated every criminal law terrain. I did cases
involving robbery, burglary, assaults, drugs and
theft. I saw political components in every trial
I did. I saw class struggle, the consequence of
poverty, the failure to provide work and education
to the destitute. I saw war on drugs as war on
the Fourth Amendment. I viewed informants as
a corruption of the truth seeking process of the
judiciary. I did entrapment trials, insanity trials,
self-defense trials, reasonable doubt trials and jury
nullification trials. The only cases I did not do were
the sexual misconduct cases; I read law, I did law;
I talked law. I learned; I experienced and grew. I
became ultimately an entanglement of plant and
bush, of tree, of branches, of vines, of crawler of
fern and flower. This was my green tropical growth
period.

At night, I chased the green neon. The Haight-
Ashbury was my center of the universe. In hats and
furs, beads and tie-dye, booted and barefooted, I
became a rock and roll dance freak; a compulsive,
acid-headed participant in the theater of gesture
on the screaming dance floors of San Francisco

hippie night scenes. Recently released from playing baseball, football and boxing at Stanford, my athletic impulses focused on the swirls and whirls of sixties music: the hand gestures, the Noh demeanors, the El Greco elongations, the vocabulary of body language in action, all the facets and forms induced by raging sound and psychedelic chemistry. By day I was a semantic warrior; by night a whirling dervish. Day and night, I was a green-hued rainbow.

My reputation spread as the winds of the time sowed my green seeds on the political paths and pastures. I was everywhere in the courts of Northern California. I would cover cases in three counties, San Francisco, Alameda and Marin, in one day. On mass arrests, I would represent a dozen arrestees at the same arraignment. I drove from court appearance to court appearance in old broken down heaps of iron that I would have to roll down hill to start the engine. My hair was long and wild, my eyes bloodshot from marijuana smoking, my suits with colorful patches on the rear, my ties flamboyant, bursting with floral splendor, my long

green tongue flitting birdlike in my pleas for bail,
for suppression of evidence, for dismissal, for not
guilty, for justice. I was as eager as a fresh green
fish splashing out of the fomenting green sea to
devour the green insects in the sea spraying air
above. I found that I could thrive on the oxygen
whirlwinds that erupted in the climate of the judicial
proceedings.

It was an era of demonstrations, protests,
heated debate, passionate speech. From the Haight-
Ashbury of San Francisco to Telegraph Avenue
in Berkeley, the hue and cry from the activist was
chanted: "No More War", "Get Out of Vietnam",
"End Police Brutality", "More Prosperity for the
Poor", "More Salary for the Farm Workers", "More
Health Service Provided", "More Food", "More
Education to the Needy", "End Racism Now",
"Power to the People". Wherever the chants
arose, I was there. Greenness was there. The
burgeoning earth shook and quaked. We roiled and
raged. Massive green shoots sprouted in the back
streets, in the fore streets, in the allrys, in the dirt,
in the asphalt, even in the cement. Cracks became

schisms; greenness was strewn in the concrete jungles; new life surged upward. We were having a rebellion. We had started a revolution.

From letter writing campaigns to legislators, to bombing the perceived enemy was the modis operandi. Radical political quasi-military groups sprang forward. Post offices, banks, gas and electric companies, oil companies were screamed at, were attacked and assaulted. Many were actually bombed. The overground press blacked out the events; the underground press bugled them.

The New World Liberation Front were the most prodigious bombing advocates. They were a national underground, multi-celled organization. They espoused open revolution, armed struggle and reform by a methodology of extortion and intimidation. They asked the energy corporations, public and private, for free fuel to the needy in winter times. If they refused, they were bombed. They asked banks for more loans to the poor; if they refused, they were bombed. They asked hospitals for free medical services to the needy; if they refused, they were bombed. Sometimes a

bank president's house was bombed. Sometimes
a government official's backyard was bombed;
sometimes the installation of Pacific Gas and
Electric was bombed. No one was hurt or killed.
NWLF wanted to take from the rich and give to
the poor. They were the Robin Hood entity of the
sixties and early seventies.

They were white; they were national; they
were well-organized; they were underground; they
were like the Black Panthers. They were Marxists
who adopted a code of direct action against the
corporate, capitalistic "pigs".

One of the most significant symbolic jury trials
of my greenhood was the twelve count criminal
case against the overground persona of the NWLF,
Jacque Rogier. A front page spectacular trial from
beginning to end. My opportunity to meet the most
influential role model of political resoluteness of my
youth. Jacque was a devout Buddhist, living near
the Haight, with a commercial printing press in his
basement. He was the Thomas Paine of the activists
of the generation. His press sparked both day and
night. He did newspapers, handouts, posters: black

and white, color, cheap paper, glossy paper. He did it free; he did it for bullets and weed; he let others author some; he wrote some; some were reprints. He and his small cadre was one of the underground oracles of the political movements of the sixties and early seventies in the San Francisco Bay Area.

He was a self-professed overground member of the NWLF. He produced their newsletter; he printed their demands; he released their secretly issued communiques to the media. He claimed he was not acquainted with the identities of the underground members. Law enforcement didn't believe him. They believed he was part of the organization's extortion efforts: he delivered the demands, the threats and participated in targeting the victims of the bombings. They charged him with twelve felony counts, boiled down to conspiracy and aiding and abetting the underground in the bombings.

He had been subpoenaed to a federal grand jury to question him on his criminal knowledge. He took a religious vow of silence. They couldn't get a word out of his mouth. The state authorities retaliated. They brought the charges. The NWLF would be exposed. Jacque would go to prison for the rest of his life. The press would be silenced; the bombing would stop.

I represented Jacque and how wrong law enforcement was in their objectives. I was a green child at a green giant's feet. Jacque masterminded the case. We defended on First Amendment principles. The only hard evidence they had was what Jacque had printed and distributed openly concerning the ideology, demands and actions of NWLF. He had never been involved in any direct action himself. He wasn't a bomber. He wasn't a lookout. He had not created the communiques. He had never attended an underground cell meeting; he was a printer of news; he had a press. He disseminated the words; he was a pacifist; he was a Buddhist.

His press ground out media press releases before and during the trial. The language of revolution, the principles of the NWLF, the political nature of his prosecution could not now be blacked out by the major media. He had created a

spiraling vortex of energy that surrounded the case.
The prosecution was depicted in colorful poster
characters of deranged buzzards devouring the First
Amendment. The posters were omnipresent.

It was the political trial of the decade for
San Francisco. The San Francisco Board of
Supervisors, even the mayor, had all received
threats from NWLF. They all became witnesses
in the trial. The case was tried in the gala-domed
City Hall of San Francisco: marble stairs; ancient,
varnished hardwood; leather seats, high ceilings
- a magnificent setting for the drama of celebrity
political images versus the outsider-the estranged,
the aberrant pamphleteer of reform and rebellion;
the gray headed, glint-eyed, academic silent monk,
Jacque Rogier.

The courtroom was standing room only;
spectators stood in the back and along the walls
of the spacious room. The press had the first few
rows. The audience had undercover police officers
as security. The hippified followers of Jacque were
like flowers among thorns. I glowed marijuana
green. Our constituency were heliotropic green,

like tender green shoots of bamboo. Our supporters were in the halls, in the streets, surrounding the City Hall, overspilling into the plaza across the street. We were like chopped celery, parsley sprinklings, green pasta in the masses of people attending the trial.

Jacque, like Huey Newton, had the greatest green force field. He stood fearlessly straight - a green cactus pole, somewhat brittle, with stickers protruding, protecting his inner juices flowing towards life's greenness. He embodied green ideas in action. He was a luminescent ray of green light - like a searchlight constantly focusing - now on the Judge, now on the District Attorney, now on his audience. The courtroom was bathed in a blinding green sheen.

Jacque was a devout disciple of the green bud cannabis. It was a sacrament for him. He provided the sacrament to all who attended court on his behalf. This was a time period when San Francisco was wide open-minded about the use of marijuana. We could smoke publicly without legal repercussion. We believed firmly that decriminalization was imminent. At Jacque Rogier's trial at the San Francisco City Hall, before and after court sessions, and at recesses, we would flood the halls - actually sit down on the floor of the hall - and some of Jacque's intimates would distribute the sacramental marijuana cigarettes. Jacque was a real cannabis expert; he selected a morning, afternoon and evening best suited strain. Morning was coffee marijuana, afternoon was tea marijuana and evening was a cocktail of green bud. This was the first and only time I conducted a jury trial stoned!

The trial consumed weeks of testimony: the defense tones vacillated from ridicule and invective to amicable pun and pleasantry. Sometimes I threw out long succulent seaweed tentacles and ensnared the opposing witness; other times I abraded them with my green cactus tongue. My eyes became green flashing jewels, but hard, obdurate and threatening luminating green fire radiation. Midway through the trial, the NWLF bombed a police patrol car parked unoccupied in front of the City Hall. The vehicle lay on its side virtually annihilated. It was a front page pictorial image that became the hub symbol of the trial. It appeared as a threat but was also an underground statement to the jury that Jacque was innocent.

In a large triumph for the First Amendment defense, Jacque Rogier was declared not guilty of the twelve criminal charges leveled against him. We had the jury polled, and each juror iterated the most precious words in criminal justice "Not Guilty" twelve times. The courtroom reverberated with 144 booming echos of "Not Guilty"; it took about half hour for the polling verdicts to be emitted, but the sound waves still splash in the consciousness of those who attended.

We were jubilant. Our followers organized a large celebration fete, a restaurant affair: food, wine, champagne, speeches. The jury was invited; most of them came. It was a gala riotous event, the sounds of uncorking champagne bottles punctuated the air. Green fluids flowed; the atmosphere scintillated with green flashing police car lights. A psychedelic, voluptuous, viscous, agua green liquid projection light show spattered the walls of the site. Hot green music and dancing hot green lava erupted; it was a wild and satisfying ceremony to our victory.

The strangest aspect of the event, however, was that Jacque Rogier did not appear; we waited and waited. Speeches were delayed. Everyone asked "Where's Jacque?" "Where's his green bud?", but he never showed up. I learned later that he had made a Buddhistic vow of monkhood if he was acquitted. Jacque had put on the yellow robe of priesthood and had gone to a mountain temple to pray. He was never seen in public again.

After the victories in Huey's and Jacque's cases, with their attendant underground and overground media projections, my personal greenness grew, flourished, expanded. My green was becoming more verdant, more intense. My green aura more visible, more prevailing, more dominant. I extended my leaves of grass from valley to hill to mountain. In the valleys I grew robust among friend and peers, within the embrace of professor and poet-sprigs of green sprang from my loins; I mated with a vibrant heliotropic force:

fertile, fecund, earth spring, a foliage in bloom. We sprouted five children, more green glittering than my eyes had heretofore beheld.

The hills were my jury trials. I traversed hill upon hill. I spread a carpet of fresh grass growth wherever I tread. I became obsessed with jury trials. I did them feverishly with fervor and fortitude. Most of the time I won. My path was ablaze with emeralds and virescent richness.

I trekked the mountains alone. The green lights and green vapors of the valleys were far below; the vivid green floodlights and searchlights of the hills could be seen, but on the peaks, seeking solitude, the cacophony of green sound and light subsided, and I communed skyward casting rays of green light to reflect upon the thin green space above. At those rare moments, I was a vegetable Moses receiving green visions of beauty and truth. I responded with all my youthful vigor to the calling of universal greenhood. I pledged myself to the struggle of oppressed people.

The next large challenge of my semantic warrior youth was the criminal trial of Russell Little

of the Symbionese Liberation Front. It was the
retrial of the brutal assassination by SLA of a Black
school superintendent, Marcus Foster. The situs of
the trial was removed to Salinas, California. The
previous trial had resulted in convictions of Little
and Romero. Little's conviction had been reversed.
The SLA was a mixed metaphor in the eyes of the
public.

SLA had captured Patty Hearst, had robbed
banks, had extorted food for the poor from
the Hearst family. They were para-military.
They believed in violent overthrow of the U.S.
government. The multi-headed cobra, their logo,
stood for justice to the underbelly of the U.S.
people by all means available. They were armed
and dangerous. Their prototype was a poster of
Patty Hearst in military uniform with machine gun
poised. They were the extremest of all movements
for social justice of the era. Marcus Foster had been
killed because he had sought to institute a program
of school IDs for ghetto area students. This was
unacceptable totalitarism for SLA, and thus the
sanction of death for its proponent.

Because Patty Hearst's father was the billionaire owner of a media empire, SLA, in kidnapping and converting her to its ideology, held the media hostage as well. Therefore, the case was widely watched by a fascinated public. The trial was removed from the immediate Bay Area to a valley agrarian environment. It was hoped that the vast pre-trial publicity of the previous case and Little's prior conviction, along with the large publicity attending the retrial, would have alighted softly on the ears of the country gentry. Nonetheless, jury selection was long and laborious because of the extreme anti-SLA bias.

Salinas, California is a small bucolic agricultural center near the Central Valley. It is an area famed for acre upon acre of patchquilt green growth: green lettuce, green spinach, green corn flourish on a green checkerboard. Green grasshoppers, green snails and green flies feed on the omnipresent verdancy. When I perceived that Salinas was engulfed in an atmosphere of pristine coloration, I realized it was our lush domain of vegetation, and I knew we could not lose. I felt myself a knight in turquoise armor.

Without being prejudiced by the harder evidence against the previous co-defendant Joe Romero, the retrial against Russell Little was one of circumstantial evidence plus a flawed identification. I was resplendent in my shimmering green armor. I spoke with wit and parable. My fingers sprouted leaves. I twirled green paper streamers in circles above the witnesses' heads the judge reflected the radiance of grassy knolls. The jury was mesmerized by green silk flags and capes. From my lips, green birds flitted and green frogs leaped. Russell Little, who stood serene and mute throughout, was duly pronounced not guilty. Joe Romero does life behind bars; his compatriot Little is flung free beyond our green pasture.

The media was dumbfounded. The front page headlines screamed "SLA Little Acquitted." The Hearst power contingent had spectated. They were rueful in their disappointment. I was marked as a counter-culture hero, but as an enemy of the establishment. A prominent and renowned criminal

defense attorney, a role model of a past generation
told me that I should retire now, that I would never
have so great a courtroom victory again, that you
obtain front page headlines only once in a lifetime,
if you are lucky, that he was envious of my success.
But he was wrong. I was at that juncture still
greenery, not yet fruit bearing. But I had indeed
harnessed the unstoppable green earth's life font
that flows powerfully, creating, sustaining and
evolving new vitalities beyond us.

These were the years that I was obtaining
the zenith of my greenhood. I was resplendent in
my green luminosity. I intuitively reached for the
sun, my leaves unfolded broadly reflecting green
rays in circles about my presence. I was green and
wet, and green wet rainbows marked my path. It
was therefore only natural that I should encounter
the winter green growth of the American Indian
Movement. The Native American is the symbol of
regenerative verdure. After winter rains, the gray,
brown, brackish earth sprouts thin, tender, fragile
shoots of grass. The freshness of the coloration
unenervates the fields and rolling hills, as the green

life force of the planet emerges once again from its dead and browned grass ancestry. There is no greater energizing earth image than the rebirth of greenery: the hair of god, the winter green grasses resurfacing on mound and meadow. Such are the Indian nations' existences: Theirs is a moonlight winter green thriving only in secretive holy places but affording a movement of coloration to our entire culture. Native American ideology is like dew crystallizing on greenery at dawn; it's gone by midday, and lies withering by afternoon sun. It was my manifest destiny that I should be drawn to the Native American. My mission was to preserve greenness, encourage and support its growth and help to extend and expand it. I was part of the green force dedicated to bring the bliss of greenness to the live planet.

Patrick "Hooty" Croy was a Northern California Indian of half Shasta and half Karuk tribes. To the Indian, the owl is like the raven is for Europeans, a messenger from after-life. Thus, "Hooty", Croy's Indian name, signified his status. He was a voice from the Great Grandfather of the Native American sub-culture, the voice from green pastures beyond life, a prophet's voice. I met him on death row in California's San Quentin Prison. His death penalty sentence for killing a white policeman had just been overturned by the California Supreme Court. He would face a retrial. I was selected by his father, a "holy man" of his tribe, to represent him in his new trial. When I first saw Hooty Croy, cuffed and shackled in a barred conference cell, he glowed of green dawn light; he appeared as a feathered, dark, ebony green owlish figure: long, black, green wings tightly curled about his body. His eyes gleamed, stoic pain emanating, fluttering green radiations. I was transfixed, held in swoon by his presence. I was not representing a human being; I was to represent a green owl deity, an animistic owl spirit whose singular gaze transfixed everything within its focus to life-giving, green rushing streams of pure, saving waters. I felt annointed in greenness.

In his first trial, "Hooty" didn't testify. He was depicted by a court-appointed lawyer as a stereotyped drunken Indian on a rampage. The lawyer begged for his life because he was out of his mind on an alcoholic binge when he murdered the dutiful police officer. Of course, he had quickly been found guilty and given the death penalty by the unsympathetic jurors. He had not trusted his lawyer; he did not testify on his own behalf; he did not even tell his lawyer that he had been shot by the officer twice from the rear before he turned and fired once in self-defense; and most saliently, the officer's bullets still lodged in his thigh and buttocks. Hooty believed at his first trial that for him it was a good time to die. In essence, he had offered no defense.

His second trial, my case, was wholly different. It became a nationally prominent Indian cause case. It was tried in San Francisco, California. Judge Stern, who presided over it, was a lifetime champion of civil rights. He saw quickly that Hooty was innocent. Owl image posters permeated the streets and underground press. Tribal leaders from throughout the U.S. attended the trial; eloquent speeches by them created an Indian rights movement around the trial. Incense burned, drums beat and chants echoed in and around the courthouse. These was "Free Hooty" walks, rallies, concerts, gatherings; Indian fried bread, grilled salmon; sacred smokings and incantations were presented at the courthouse. The ambiance was a great swelling vapor of green puffing power. This Indian cause case could not be overlooked.

The opening statement that flew like green birds and butterflies from my mouth became the refrain and chant of the case: "This is a case about a police officer who shot an Indian in the back"; "this is a case about a drunk police officer who shot an Indian in the back"; "This is a case about a drunk police officer who shot an Indian in the back during a cease fire." Yes, it had turned out that the officer's blood alcohol was beyond the legal limit. He had been called to duty from his day off. He had come to the scene of the police-Indian stand-off under the influence. Also, he had snuck up on Hooty during an official police announced cease fire period so that negotiations could occur. During that time, Hooty, with a .22 hunting rifle, had come down to his aunt's cabin to see if she had been shot;

he was climbing in the window when the officer, out of bounds during the cease fire, came around the corner of the cabin and shot Hooty in the rear as he attempted to crawl in the window. Hooty had instinctively turned and let off one shot in self-defense reaction. The bullet, guided by the hand of providence, went into the heart of the police officer. The so-called shootout was four Indians with one old rifle versus about three dozen police armed liked a militia shooting to kill. The police were massacre-minded. The Indians were involved only in their survival. The "Not Guilty" by the jury resounded in the Indian culture like bells and bugles of vindication. The case is presently a Hollywood movie. Owls still adorn my office walls.

The case also created a legalistic novelty which has added to a national defense theme: we presented with the good guidance of the Court, what is called a "cultural defense". We were allowed to explain by historical evidence why the four Indians ran from the police instead of surrendering at the beginning. (There was a police vehicle pursuit; the Indians had taken refuge on a hill behind Hooty's aunt's cabin located in the foothills of the Sierras in Northern California.) We showed the jury by a parade of Native American forensic experts that the Pacific Northwest Indian tribes had been genocided by the white settlers, miners and military between 1850 and 1900. We showed the atrocities of the genocide: the killing and burning of Indian villages, women and children; the poisoning of the Indians, the implanting of tuberculosis in their tribes; the seizures of their land and property; their present day plight of unemployment and lack of education. When we finished with our cultural defense, there were scant dry eyes in the courtroom. We had covered everyone and muted their emotions with a blanket of the thick green moss of Indian pain and suffering.

The Patrick Hooty Croy cultural defense inspired minorities around the country to utilize the theme in criminal cases involving racism, discrimination and genocide. Our briefs were sent to lawyers in the south and in the north. Hooty had indeed struck a blow for his ancestry against white man's historical oppression of the red and black peoples of America.

Hooty lives among the giant Sequoia Redwoods in Northern California now, a freed spirit. He hoots green sounds in nighttime darkness under the largest most verdant canopy on the continent.

The Hooty case wrapped me in a silken cape of forest green leaves. I earned an eagle feather for my lawyer's role in struggling for him and Native Americans in general. The feather remains my panache even today. Our Indian paralegals and Indian expert witnesses remain my green brothers and sisters. The jury that acquitted Hooty meets for lunch annually to celebrate their act of justice.

My next large case took me to Miami, Florida - a choking humid atmosphere of burgeoning tropical vegetation repressed by urban edifice construction. I saw frenzied green ants, and green flies and green spiders in hectic scramble upon steel concrete and neon.

I was defending a high ranking Mafia member from New York City accused of attempted murder, extortion and racketeering. I took the case to establish a national identity. A green force from San Francisco hippydom fighting for the soul of gangland alleged killer: a mixed karma metaphor from any perspective. This case posed the greatest challenge to my greenhood. I felt myself to be a Green Knight of the West in mortal combat with a Red Knight of the South. I went as a Crusader for the green cause, for the dominancy of green over red.

Red was a threat to green. Red was violence: the slashing of flesh in battle, the blood flowing wounds of social disorder, the coagulation of the life force and the petrifying of its victims. Red rendered a culture death and destruction. Green is the life force perpetually opposing red, the death force. The Mafia case in Miami would be a chromatic struggle of opposing colors: the green tentacles of spreading humanism and compassion reaching above and around the flooding of bleeding lacerations imposed by red knights on numerous court battle fields.

I served the green surge, the first perceived premise of planetary life infusing organic growth in its myriad forms upon the inorganic sub-structure of the universe. Green is truth, beauty, health, recovery and restoration. It's the only color that can vanquish the dark, crimson hue of extracted and strangled life forms. I, a green defense lawyer versus a red prosecutor, a leaf of green pitted against a scabbing, festering wound; a green rainbow fighting in a metaphysical contest with a blood streaked rapier.

And what a trial drama ensued! Under the eyes of the legal patricians of Miami, with the bellicose voice of my client at my rear, I fought with an unleashed fury unknown to me in previous litigations. I was promised by the local lawyer establishment a marble bust of my likeness in their Hall of Justice if I could win this impossible case. They viewed me with a smug satire.

The client was a thug of a man, oxen bodied and oxen minded. He had nearly killed one of his own species by a brutal baseball bat beating. The prosecutor opened his case by playing a recording made by the victim where the defendant, in a baritone growl, said "You should be dead." The

battered victim was cooperating with the police.
He had fallen significantly behind in his "juice"
(interest) payments on a shark loan. He was to
be "hit" as an example. He had nowhere to hide;
he had turned state's evidence after being in a
prolonged, near-death coma. The evidence gave
graphic accounts of the underlying activities
that had prompted the attack: the loan sharking
operation, the methods and structure of the "mob",
the secret gambling casino lifestyles of the Miami
area, clandestine opulent hotel meetings, the passing
of bundles of one hundred dollar bills. The FBI had
put a recording device under the bed of a Miami
Mafia Captain in charge of the areas gambling and
loan operations. Confidences had been penetrated.
The victim had been a "made man" himself, and his
debriefings had exposed the entire illegal operations
of the New York City crime family in Southern
Florida. A book would be written to document this
early inside perspective of Miami organized crime.

The prosecutor was confident, brilliant red
self-esteem. The Judge was an ex-FBI, unabashed,
red-biased against us. Every day I fought the

Judge more than the prosecutor. The defense bar was aligned with the red forces, mainly because I was from the outside green world and I vigorously resisted the opposing force. Like many areas across the country, the defense bar was on the norm, passive and acquiescent to the prosecution: a class of dilettante legal professionals, praying to and prey of Mammon.

The strategy of our defense case was an appeal to jury nullification. The defendant couldn't testify. His long Mafia past actions would be exposed. He had in essence confessed his guilt in the recorded telephone conversations. He was obviously guilty. But law enforcement had overreached. They had KGBed the investigation. Their vices were the vices of a totalitarian government. It was transparent that they even had the Judge in their pocket. I compared the FBI investigation to a Stalin or SS Hitler-type of military process: the use of compromised informants deriving large benefits from the government, the unbridled use of electronic eavesdropping, from recorded calls to bedroom intimate conversations; the use of secret video recordings, the sneaks and peeks by undercover police; the land and airplane surveillances. I wanted the jury to be the true conscience of the community, to say to the FBI that the conviction was less important than the curtailing of police state tactics. The case for me involved the weighing of the evils: the evil of the Mafia mentality versus the evil of the secret police state methods. I tried to occupy the higher moral ground. I asked for a verdict based on comparative moral values rather than evidence. It was the typical jury nullification theme but dressed anew in Mafia versus FBI metaphors. I put on trial, not the defendant, but the vice of government.

The case went beyond the mere stereotypical clash of inequities. There were profound issues. The government wanted to frame the trial into the eternal platitude of the good guys versus the bad guys, the cops vs. the crooks. The prosecution relies on the public's conditioned response to this cartooned version of societal reality. It is this over simplification that destroys jury impartiality and ultimately the jury system itself. The calling of the case was to expose and break down this false dichotomy.

The Mafia, it was shown, is a subculture, a microcosmic social, economic and political unit sufficient unto itself. It has a hierarchy, a value system, a governing body and a justice proceeding that mirrors our dominant culture, but exists and operates independent of the majority. It seldom visits harm outside its social and economic borders. It has its own system of rewards and punishments. It is truly an alternate culture. The philosophic question posed to the jury as a consequence of the above was by what authority does the law of the majority apply to a minority living outside of the majority's society? Should sophisticated law doctrine extend to a more primitive sub-culture? For what is true and just in the demi-mode, can such be amenable to externally applied standards, judgments and sanctions? Boiled down to basics, what right do we have to imprison the cannibal? The trial placed great stress on my greenness. Was I being naive, quixotic? Was the undertaking a fool's errand? Was my green torchlight dimming? Was I just a Haight-Ashbury summer storm, green flower quick to rise, quick to perish in the red glow of the heat of a larger truth?

I took refuge during the trial in a tranquil turquoise sea. Florida waters were streaked and speckled with green glitter at dawn. I would bathe in the chartreuse fluid cosmos at dawn each day. I had to recharge, renovate, reinvigorate my green vitality. The green streaking skies at sunrise was a time where greenness prevailed without conflict. I saw no rosy cloud to mar my visions. I walked the early morning naked beaches. I sought out exotic greens to reinforce my fortitude. Green tortoises rose from the sea to greet me; green parrots flew above, green crabs at my feet, green fish in the waves, green palm trees lined my path; green shrimp for breakfast. They all cuddled and cradled my pristine coloration; they infused belief and strength into my being. Greenish morning mists swelled over me. I became armed with a green obsidian semantic spear. My final closing argument thundered with green lightening flashing from the podium. I could not lose the case.

The jury was unable to return a verdict. The case hung ten to two for guilty. Two jurors who had seen what had happened in Nazi Germany could not endorse the FBI's means and methods. They had nullified a guilty verdict. They had dissented from endorsing American Government overreach into the personal privacy and liberties of its citizens. The case was never retried. The Mafia client returned to New York City. It was a victory. I jokingly asked for two-twelfths of a sculptured bust in the courthouse. The ex-FBI federal judge retired soon after. The green seas of the Florida coast swelled over the shores and land that night.

I was later asked by the same family to represent more of them in New York City, to come to New York to re-establish my base there, in reality to become a Mafia lawyer. Anything that I wanted would be mine. They had treated me well. I was a green grass-fed hippie from San Francisco and must remain a free spirit in order to follow the green trails away from the dark woods of man's inhumanity to man.

J. Tony Serra

The most difficult metaphor for me to absorb
in my green years, the early years of my life and
practice of law is that dirt is dead grass: that Earth,
soil, humus, the matrix of life forms, is merely
dust unto dust; that it is the decayed, mutilated,
granulated, shrunk, shriveled and trod upon residue
of all spring greenery that glorifies the earth; that
from the collective winter corpse of all verdure
and green foliage springs the vivid rebirth of the
vegetable kingdom. In Waco, Texas, defending
a major drug transaction defendant, I learned
that death is an important part of life's cycle; that
green life must die to regenerate further green life;
then green re-incarnates green. Any epiphany in
the Waco defeat was that I must lose to win, that
withered green does not with finality perish: that
guilty verdicts are the endless rocking of the cradle
of non-guilty verdicts.

In the Waco case, my client, a famously
successful architect and builder, traded kilos
of cocaine for money and marijuana. It was a
governmental sting operation. The defense was the
defense of entrapment.

My first impression of Waco is that it was sepulchral. It was a dead zone, brown, flat and sterile; utterly devoid of greenery. A heavy gray sky hung low over the town like a curtain draped over dead people. It was located on the first circle of Dante's Inferno. The center piece of Waco was the courthouse where the jury trial was to take place: it was a magnificent edifice of past and faded glory. Encircled by brown and demised lawns, it stood like a cemetery monument, domed with archangels perched standing in the structure blowing horns for Judgment Day. The town itself was divided between the bourgeois and the impoverished. It was a sanctimonious subculture. Dry sun bleached churches with their dry sun bleached parishioners on one side-at the other end of town, alcoholism, depression, bars and bawdy music. Over all the pallor of doom covered in dead leaves and dried skeletons of vines and bush. There was nothing lush: no birds, no frogs, no butterflies, no youth, no laughter; only the old and the discarded silently begging for green life.

J. Tony Serra

I early walked the dark stubble of the outskirts of town. I encountered a farmer-type. We were talking. A greenish grasshopper labored through the dryness, crawling awkwardly. The Waco denizen without concern or forethought, stamped it into the dust, squished its life into the earth with his heavy dirty boot. We went on conversing as if nothing had happened. I derived from this symbolism that my green force, the aura of vivacity that engulfed me, would find its defeat here in Waco, Texas.

Entrapment in a drug case is the defense of last resort. The accused admits he did the crime but argues that he had no prior disposition to do it and was induced into the transaction by law enforcement. What an entrapped defendant is saying to the jury is that he has been a victim of police-created crime, that the police inculcated the intent to provide the drug in the defendant's mind, that ultimately the entrapped defendant is the unwitting agent of police actions. The defense of entrapment is well established in the law books and in the court decisions, but the general lay populace doesn't like it – it's lawyer double talk; if a person commits a crime, who cares who started the idea goes the refrain from the masses. In many, especially in southern states, the defense of entrapment is untenable.

And this trial in Waco, Texas was in Bible-Belt territory, a fundamentalistic Baptist, red-neck domain; no tolerance for deviance, no compassion, no mercy. The judicial system was one huge black spider pouncing on every fly or insect trapped in its web of litigation. A culture that lives on a staple of meat and eggs has very little appetite for spinach and lettuce. I realized that I could not bring greenery to all patches of the earth. Every day of the trial, the green clover and leek, the sage and corn stalk, the green hummingbirds and dragonflies that emanated from my throat, melted death-like upon contact with the torpid vapors of the courtroom.

My client testified on his own behalf. He was strong and solid like the expensive homes and stylish architecture he created. He told the jury how he had overexpanded in his construction business, that he had become cash flow short, how

the governmental agent had lured him to Texas for
a one-time, big cocaine deal. He knew a source
for kilos; the source would take marijuana as well
as money for the drugs. He was desperate for
the cash. The undercover agent was providing
marijuana and cash; he couldn't be the DEA. They
would never trade illegal substances for illegal
substances. My client was honest, forthright and
endearing. The government had manipulated him;
the DEA had created a false safe house front replete
with recreational drug use and seductive young
women; he had been duped. It was a classical
case of entrapment. He pleaded to the jury for a
second chance. He had worked long and honestly,
legally and law-abiding all of his life. He had made
a positive contribution to society; he had hired
hundreds of workers and paid them top wages.
His houses were beautiful; he was admired and
respected in the building trade community. He
would have never committed the crime, but for the
allurements of the DEA. He had been stung. He
was not really a criminal. He had deep remorse.
He would never step over the line again.

The courtroom was crowded; the Baylor Law School students came to watch the case. When the defendant testified, there was an eerie silence that enveloped the room. Some law students nodded in understanding and empathy. When the jury retired, I learned that the Judge, the clerk, the law students, the local lawyers and the experienced court watchers were all for "not guilty." For them, we had fulfilled the standard for exoneration by entrapment. But the jury was cold, punitive, harsh and vindictive; they quickly and easily convicted him. There is no defense of entrapment in the lay, rustic, religious mentality of Waco, Texas.

His life destroyed, his business ruined, his family abandoned, the defendant commenced a long prison term. Somehow he escaped, through guile or consideration, only later to be gunned down by a young rookie policeman in the San Francisco-Bay Area. Law enforcement, who had set their trap in Texas, received their pound of flesh in California. He had secreted out of Waco jail a jumpsuit inmate's uniform and had given it to me as a memento during the trial. It's white with black lettering on the back. I have it still.

I was invited by the Judge much later to attend a law conference in Austin at which I was to be honored by presentation of a Texas long brimmed cowboy hat, a booby prize of a sort. I never attended: no victory, no celebration.

I had carried my own lawyer's corpse back to San Francisco. I made haste to replenish my earth-given green force by battling in local cases, one after the next, in a near frenzy to achieve renewal. My wounds, inflicted at Waco, became scars, and the scars became strengths. The damage to my lush period receded once again. Green mastery fulfilled its prophesy. I was a tall, shimmering eucalyptus tree.

The Yellow Years

~

As imperceptibly as spring transmutes to summer, I flowed from green to yellow. Much later in the fullness of my golden years, it was obvious to me that I was adorned in gilded raiment and tread beneath showers of sun flung gold, but the early transition phase, being unanticipated, took me unaware. Lying in verdant clover, cleansing in morning mist, nestled in plant and grass, I glimpsed a change in my bodily hues; the green moss fuzz covering my skin was turning yellowish; my grass green hair flecked now with gold-dust sparkle; my eyes emitted fire yellow; I felt my aura glowing golden rays of energy. In several months my greenhood evolved into yellowness. I stood a golden eagle with golden crown ready for flight.

I had become a mature semantic warrior, with armature of gold, begilded sword and voice that was a rush of yellow feathered arrows. Green

parrots and green hummingbirds that had once
surrounded me became yellow canaries and golden
finches. Green bamboo became yellow cornfields;
marijuana plants turned to sunflowers; green
flies to yellowjacket bees; green apples to yellow
plums. Butter and egg yolks nourished me in lieu
of vegetable and salad. I gathered to my bosom
the poppy, marigold and goldenrod and walked no
longer amidst the green succulents and virid flora.
My jewels became of gold rather than emerald.

Likewise my mind ripened to accommodate
my golden age. I swelled with sunlight and radiated
both prose and poem. My bloom of florid charisma
spilled over into and occupied the contiguous
spheres of the political and the societal. I was no
longer the green lawyer knight. I was now intensely
bright and emblazoned, flaring and forceful. I
had transformed, mutated, to a brilliant chromatic
metaphor in pursuit of justice for all downtrodden
people, a whirling dervish of sun streams casting
golden verbiage to a subculture seeking freedoms
and fairness.

J. Tony Serra

I traversed near and far, from judicial environment to social, to political, didactic and clandestine forums. I raged and reasoned on behalf of egalitarianism. I became a speaker, an orator. These times in our cultural history, the eighties required a gilt-robed spectacle to champion the reform movements of minority inequality. I was thus among the chosen. Many fiery torches appeared throughout the U.S. to light; each of us had the power of our rich, glaring colorific energy. My role as the erupting volcano from the criminal justice system was to pour my molten lava on those societal motifs that sought to extinguish the constitutional and civil rights of the U.S. citizenry.

Accordingly, I allowed myself to expand to national prominence. Impassioned speeches were presented to lawyer conventions all over California, Oregon, Washington, Colorado, Idaho, Utah, Texas, Ohio, Florida, Georgia, New Jersey, New York and Washington D.C. My subject matter varied but the common thread was that my presentations were always anti-establishment, anti-government. I spoke literally hundreds of times and railed against racism, informants, mandatory sentences, preventative detention, fourth amendment abuses and prosecutorial misconduct. I made equally emotional presentations furthering the causes of decriminalization of drugs, enactment of medical marijuana statutes, jury nullification; how to cross-exam effectively informants, jury voir dire methods in minority defendant cases, and the giving of anti-government closing arguments. Every subject upon which I spoke came from vivid courtroom experiences I had collected in my greenhood period. I knew the law; I knew juries; I was a hammer and a fist of words and symbols.

My caseload in my middle years was extraordinary. I became celebrated as a "back to back" jury trial specialist. I selected juries while waiting for jury verdicts in the preceding case. It was routine for me to work on dozens of cases at the same time. I flayed my golden tongue east, west, north and south in the U.S. I did cases in over 40 U.S. jurisdictions: Tennessee, Georgia, Florida, Texas, South Carolina, in the South; New York, New Jersey, Vermont, in the East; Illinois,

Minnesota, Ohio, Montana, Idaho, Washington D.C.
in the North; and California, Nevada, Utah, Oregon,
Washington, Hawaii in the West. I won most of
my cases. I had burst like a giant yellow sunflower
nurtured in legalese of the trial courts blooming in
the sunshine of media attention.

I was allowed space on radio, TV and in
the print media. I participated in Black, Indian,
Hispanic and Asian cause cases; political cause
cases, environmental cause cases, and drug
cause cases. I did murder; I did conspiracy. I
did racketeering; I did smuggling. I did drug
manufacturing; I did prison gangs and Hell's
Angels; I did SLA; I did Earth First. I did animal
rights activists; I did countless insanity and
diminished capacity cases. I threw my rain of gold
into the infernos of broiling conflict. I experienced,
I learned, I yellowed, I goldened, I spoke, I taught;
I raved and bellowed for the underdog. Awards
and commendations were bestowed upon me from
many directions. As I write, I have been acclaimed
trial attorney of the year twice and runner-up trial
attorney of the year once. I have appeared in at

least 40 different jurisdictions throughout the United States.

From the other side, the status quo, the government, the political conservative's perspective, I was an insurrectionist. I was jailed more times for contempt of court than any other known trial attorney. I refused to pay federal income tax and have suffered three misdemeanor, non-moral turpitude convictions for my refusal, resulting in federal prison sentences on two occasions. Each time my license to practice has been suspended but not revoked. My outlawism in regard to tax boycott is an issue of principle, not criminality, so that my golden image was blurred but not tarnished. During my yellowhood, I stood strong and straight, a semantic warrior, sculpted from a monolith of solid gold.

My symbolic cases of that era were manifold. The most singular burst of sun energy was the federal racketeering trial of the Hell's Angels in San Francisco, California. Over twenty-five Hell's Angels members of many jurisdictions had been indicted on RICO charges. The United

States Attorney's Office considered the Club as an international organized crime entity, a violently controlling monopoly of the manufacturing and distribution of methamphetamine. By their use of the so-called Racketeering Statute, the federal government sought to have life sentences imposed on the most notorious of the Angels' members, and to accomplish total annihilation of the Clubs' assets by forfeiture. The goal of the prosecution was complete destruction of this motorcycle organization.

Many dozen search and seizure warrants were served on clubhouses and members' homes. They were unique in that they were called "indicia" warrants: anything manifesting Hell's Angels' "indicia" could be seized and forfeited. Club colors, logos and expressions appearing on their motorcycles, vehicles, private property, clothing, tools, clubhouse mementos, photos, documents, practically everything that members proudly displayed, were confiscated by law enforcement. The government took the Clubs' money, bank accounts, records, membership lists, maps, minutes of the meetings, even their trophies. From the view of the DEA, ATF and FBI, these items were the spoils of their declared war against Hell's Angels. These warrants signaled their invasion and conquest of the Club.

Law enforcement did not understand that the myth of the Hell's Angels was as essential to the dream of American freedoms as the myth of the American cowboy. Hell's Angels were poetry on wheels. They remain the quintessential symbol of liberty at large. The roar of their road glory is the metaphor of all of our personal freedoms. Their rights are our rights. A Hell's Angel speeding loudly down the highway on the back of a Harley Davidson is an enduring image of Americana cherished by generations of emancipated minds.

The prosecution was in flagrant bad faith. They had, by bringing these inflated prosecution charges, sought the oblivion of an American icon. It was overkill; it was doomed for failure.

There were so many defendants in court; there was such an enormous witness list that the Judge ordered "witness books" for the jury. Each book contained photographs of all defendants and each major witness so that the jury had a memory aid that connected them to the evidence presented over such a long, protracted, disjointed trial. The court was daily packed with many motorcycle club members and afficionados - mostly tough, virile, bawdy in appearance; but strong, silent and protest images by their presence. The case was of national prominence, covered daily by TV and print media.

The trial was the Olympic event of all jury trials. It was my first big battle as a luminous yellow egg yolk. I bulged and swelled florid golden textures of fire and light from my central globe to the perimeters of the courtroom. The court became a huge canary feathered crown. I stood in its center, begilded with flames of the burning torch in my grasp. I poured hot molten sun, brilliant verbiage on the throne of the jury box. It was a Shakespeare play in a courtroom performed under glowing melting sunshine. We were bathed in rains of gold. There was not one overcast or rainy day.

The trial, like most politically motivated trials, contained a parade of perjurious informants compromised by law enforcement pressures and given vast benefits of money and leniency for their own admitted crimes. Immunity for murders, drug violations, assaults and robberies was the chief reward to the snitches. One received $30,000 cash in a closed suitcase from a law enforcement officer. These witnesses, the mainstay against most defendants, were literally laughed at by the jury.

It was a six month trial. The podium turned golden to my touch. I became the warrior for warriors. I brought the rush and noise of motors into the courtroom. I poured the legend and the glory of emblazoned yellow Hell's Angels into the jury box. We all - the defendants, the lawyers, the judge, the jury - scintillated in the court's crown of radiating goldenness.

My client was the most perfect symbol of the free Angel spirit. He was a mechanical minded genius. His centered love of life was his motorcycle and the open road. He despised wealth and possessions. I had a photo of him straddled on his bike on a remote desert road, dirty and swaggering with virility. I blew it up to 4 x 6 feet, put it on a

placard and waved it in the jury's face at closing
argument. "This is the face of the American Dream;
this is not the face of a Racketeer," I screamed.
The jury agreed. All racketeering charges against
all Angels were found to be "not guilty." The
indicia assets were returned to them. It was a
great victory for personal freedoms in the United
States. I still see the Harley Davidsons, dozens
and dozens of them, lined up on the street in front
of my law office. During the trial, we met there
each afternoon. All Angels not in custody and
uncharged members, the lawyers, the investigators,
our witnesses, and well wishers. The red and black
colors, the death heads on leather jackets, worn-
out boots, bearded men with large fists, gruff and
growling: they merged with me in a yellow ray
of sun gold for the common cause of freedom and
justice. Flakes and spangles of yellow light still
illuminate in my memory of those blazing days!

My transition to richness and fullness of my
florid yellow era had been accomplished. As my
green years grew strength within me, yellow was
my powerful time of being. Green was growth;

yellow was bloom. Green was seeing and feeling; yellow was illuminating and glaring. Green was sowing; yellow was harvesting. Green was intelligence; yellow was knowledge. I became a sun refracting, gold-armored word warrior always forward charging on my gilded steed. Whereas previously the green earth was my sustenance, now the kiss and bliss of sunshine lifted my spirit.

I rode up on billowy gold-tinged clouds to Baltimore, Maryland to do battle with the Federal DEA for the freedom of a Lebanese Christian - a government high ranking phalangist in the government of Lebanon, and an admitted vastly wealthy hashish distributor at the international level. He was locked dungeon-like in an ancient stone prison on the outskirts of the City. I was his knight from San Francisco who would free him. It was a case with scenarios from many locations. We would visit by testimonial evidence the hashish industry of rural Lebanon; the island of Cyprus, the Mediterranean waters offshore of Egypt; Lisbon, Portugal; a bank in San Francisco, and ultimately, the alleged hub of the import scheme, Baltimore,

Maryland. It was a jury trial that taxed the imagination of the participants. It was historical, political and involved higher dimensions of morality and ethics.

Baltimore was barren earth and dissolutive citizenry; a dry and dreary urban atmosphere. My mission was to restore and redeem, to uplift and emancipate not only my client, but the ambiance of the criminal justice system itself.

My client's lineage from before the birth of Christ had been involved in the making and selling of hashish. Hashish was entwined with religion and social life in Lebanon. It was not only legal, it was sacrament. The oils of annointment was the elixir of the hashish. Marijuana fields were cultivated century upon century for its production. Hashish making was in that country and others of the Middle East, a time-honored and respected profession and industry. The DEA had entrapped the industry's tycoon, brought him to the United States for the purpose of imprisoning him for life. What was legal in Lebanon, what was prized and nurtured there, was like poison in the United States, and the federal government in its arrogant omnipotence had sought a trophy in its international war on so-called drugs.

The obvious defense was entrapment. An informant agent of the DEA had been sent to Lebanon to negotiate for boatloads of hashish to be sent to Egypt, to be sent to Sicily, to be brought to the USA. The client did what he had done for his lifetime: he sold; he delivered. He was an honest and forthright merchant of hashish. He showed the undercover agent the fields of growing marijuana, the factories where the buds were converted into hashish. He was proud of his enterprise and of his product. He was doing nothing illegal or morally wrong in his country. He was flown in a lavishly furnished private jet to the United States for the monetary payment: he was brought to a bank; the money was counted and he was arrested. It had been a DEA setup, a ploy, a game plan of deceit. The professional informant/agent playing the role of the buyer and distributor had manipulated the Lebanese merchant and brought him to his captors. The agent was paid handsomely for

the performance; the U.S. government gloated;
conservative Baltimore would convict, and the U.S.
government would have "taken out" a General, in
their minds, in the war on drugs.

It was into such atmosphere I came to
champion the cause of justice. What a person does
lawfully in his own country cannot be punished
in another; a basic maxim that only the despots of
empire building violate. I was a complete alien in
Baltimore: a glittering hippie goldenrod from San
Francisco treading upon the dry blanched, dead
earth of Maryland. My client held captive by the
cringing brown dust and death of the environment.
The life forces in Baltimore were at nadir, and the
human condition reflected it.

Manifestations of racism and poverty were
pervasive blotches on the topography. The social
ethos flowing into the court's legal system was
introverted, dull and droll: no animation; no
spontaneity; a sun forsaken and sun abandoned
land, lacking both green and yellow images of
generation and fruition. But I had come from the

sky; I was a sun god; I brought the blush of yellow warmth to the dying sphere.

The client was religious, prayerful, hoping for his God's mercy but stoic and accepting. He possessed unlimited assets; he tried to select the best lawyers in America. He obtained, as my local counsel, a Washington D.C. criminal specialist of renown reputation. He told me confidentially that no one wins on the defense side in Baltimore. He charged a huge fee; he lived in a mansion; his passion was breeding show horses. He asked me to visit with him there. I didn't. I was in my prime; he was in decline as a trial attorney. I did most everything. I visited with the client daily, even on weekends. I cross- examined their star informant/ agent witness; I gave the closing argument. The co-counsel foresaw a crushing defeat; he wanted to project the fault toward me. Of course, he had never encountered a flash of yellow streaking lightning from California.

The federal courtroom in Baltimore was relatively unique in that the witness chair was not located elevated by the side of the Judge's bench,

like in most courts. The witness was seated on
a wooden upright chair on the floor level in the
center of the court area. The witness was therefore
surrounded by court personnel: the Judge, the
clerks, the lawyers, the jury and closer to the
defendant than usual. The witness was in full
display; usually the lower body is hidden by the
witness "stand", but here the legs and feet and all
body movement was open and potent to the jury's
observation. For me, it was a great advantage; I
could circle the witness; I could fling my darts and
arrows from all perspectives; I could withdraw
from him body language responses that were clear
to the jury: his flinches, leg shaking, his drooping,
hunching and fidgeting were all clearly on review. I
knew that if I could destroy the credibility of their
star witness, we could secure victory.

I don't believe that my feet touched the ground
during the entirety of the six week trial. I danced,
I dashed, I flew. I floated like a giant, wild canary,
always with a blazing fireball sun rising from my
rear. Sometimes into the court seeped yellow
molten-flowing lava; sometimes a hue of golden

mist, sometimes spiraling waves of splashing blond waters. I plied in view of jury gilded pineapples, yellow peaches, sun kissed yellow mangoes. I showed them the yellow of crow's foot and straw, of butter and yolk, of goldfish and goldfinch. Yellow tobacco smoked the courtroom and tall sunflowers bloomed in the aisles. I became King Midas; I turned the courtroom into gold. The jury was bathed in a colorific halo, a rainbow of all shades and tones of yellowness. The courtroom, all attaches, the audience of spectators, all of us, rose heavenly upward floating on golden spectrummed clouds.

I burned hot fire for three hours during closing argument. I emitted jagged, splicing flames; yellow hot sparks and fire pieces emanated from my roaring furnace. The jury was emblazoned by my incendiary verbal deluge. I screamed, pretended the situation was reversed. Pretend in his country television was poison: TVs were banned and illegal and the possession or sale of them there was a serious crime. Pretend he came to the United States and bought a boatload of TVs. Pretend he asked the TV corporate president to fly to Beirut to pick up the money in payment for them. Pretend that the Lebanese authorities arrested our TV Executive for selling TVs. "Would you find him guilty?" Of course, the jury said "no". The phalangist from Lebanon was acquitted. A miracle in Baltimore had occurred.

My next memory was a lavish freedom celebration dinner in Washington D.C. My co-counsel, the client's family, an appreciative client, all assembled before he chauffeured to Montreal and boarded a French Concorde jet to Paris. I was offered a free trip to vacation at his mansion in Cyprus; I was given a credit card in his name to use in the future in any way I deemed appropriate. I was asked to visit him in Lebanon. I never did any of it; I rejoiced privately supplicating myself to the golden altar of yellow flaming justice and giving thanks for my bright luster.

Wherever I tread in this golden age time of life, my path was paved with golden leaf. I glowed and glittered in yellow sunlight. I was a bubbling font of sun streaming liquid. It was an era of

surplus, of excess, of ornate art and architecture.
I was the sculpted gold-plated semantic warrior
standing proudly, radiating, flaunting, flaring,
flaming, glaring and casting blinding sun reflections
in all directions. I was an exploding star of
daylight. My cup spilled viscous gold over its brim;
I was adorned in gold vestments embroidered with
gold threads. Televison, radio, public and lawyers'
forums opened their arms for my presence. I was
enshrined, encircled by friends and admirers. My
grandiosity became near quixotic.

Amidst this flow of my mid-years came a call
from the "gold country" of California: a mother
had rescued her child from a dragon monster and
was in mortal peril. A damsel called in distress to
gilded Sir Lancelot to protect her. This was the call
of the media famous Ellie Nestler case; a call from
Sonora, California, the gold nuggeted, gold specked
foothills of California - sacks of gold in the banks,
gold nuggets in the rivers, gold dust flowing in
the winds; a golden opportunity for a golden hued
warrior of the courts.

Ellie Nestler had shot dead her young son's child molester in a courtroom during a recess from his preliminary hearing. Her child had been scheduled to testify against this serial child abuser, but had collapsed in a froth of tears, too fearful of the man to go forward. The molester, confident of his escape from justice, had "smirked" at both her and her child, implying in the knowing smile that he would be free to sexually assault the boy again. The smirk pitched Ellie over the edge. God "told her" it was all right to kill this evil man and she had gone to her vehicle, retrieved a handgun, returned to court and emptied it into the victim.

First in the foothills of California, then throughout the nation, she became a folk hero for vigilante justice, a woman's rights advocate and had blossomed into a public speaker for the cause: the courts had not been severe enough on child molesters. They were recidivistic; mothers had the natural right to protect their children when courts and law enforcement had failed. Ellie was a heroine, not a criminal. Children sex victims should not have to openly testify in courts; "Free Ellie" became the hue and cry of the domain.

Ellie Nestler was annointed in supportive publicity. She had become a "talking head" television personality. She was articulate and determined. She invaded the higher moral ground of the issues. Where the prosecution wanted first degree murder, the local populace gave her cheers, parades, accolades and blessings. Rains of gold descended on her path.

Ellie wanted honest justice. She did not want vigilante justice; she did not want jury nullification; she did not believe that a person could take justice in her own hands; she did not believe that anyone had the right to kill. She had been a victim herself of childhood molestation; the terrible "smirk" had precipitated a temporary psychosis. God had told her it was all right to exterminate this evil one. For her, it was a simple, direct, clear cut case of not guilty by reason of temporary insanity. I agreed and that was her defense offered at jury trial.

The courthouse, a wooden gabled, antique structure was set high upon a knoll that rose

mysteriously upward from the main street of
Sonora. One looked up at the courthouse from the
street; it appeared castle-like above low trees that
lay beneath it. It truly symbolized the grand edifice
of justice in that small town. Citizens lined the
streets carrying placards displaying "Free Ellie" and
"We love you, Tony." Bumper to bumper vehicles
sounded horns as they passed by. TV antennaed
vans were parked curbside. It was a media circus.
We would stroll through the crowds and reporters
and TV cameras at the comings and leavings of
court sessions. The underlying facts of the case
were not much in dispute; it was to be a battle of
the psychiatrists. The courtroom was packed to
capacity every single day of trial.

Our case centered around two chief metaphors;
Ellie had reacted blindly and instinctively like a
"she-bear" protecting her cub", and her mind's flow
had disintegrated like water "spilling over the rapids
or falls of a roaring river." I argued vigorously that
she was not legally responsible for her actions; she
was literally "out of her mind" at the time of the
events. It was a "six shrink" litigation.

Every night of the trial, I communed with solar energy. I infused my spirit with rays of sun and moon yellowness. My corn cob pipe sent up billowing, circling, light-lit yellow smoke signals from burning, blond Lebanese hashish. I smoked ritualistically, summoning the muses in my aid.

The jury compromised. They brought in a verdict of manslaughter. Ellie did about two years in prison and was released. Breast cancer had appeared during trial. Her head was shaved; chemotherapy was applied in prison. The cancer was arrested. But Ellie's spirit broke. Her son became truant and vicious. He was later convicted of cruelly murdering a helpless old man. Ellie was later returned to prison for five years on drug offenses. She, who had risen to great heights of public image, from mishap and misfortunate, plummeted downward to even more painful depths of mishap and misfortune. Another legend had been lost.

But when I strode away from the hills of the gold country, my golden mantle and fiery torch still served me well.

J. Tony Serra

From the rolling hills of Sonora, I pranced sunlight and luminous to the rolling hills of Mendocino County, to the emerald triangle of Northern California to the solar-bathed, lush vineyards and marijuana fields near Ukiah, California. A sheriff deputy had been killed in an alleged shootout with renegade Indians on a reservation. The responsible Indian youth had fled and was hiding in the mountains. A death penalty charge had been filed. The defendant's name was "Bear" Lincoln.

I had been approached in San Francisco by his cousin, a massive Native American tribal leader, proud and strong and honest, scarred both physically and emotionally by many battles with white authorities. His words were his absolute integrity. He told me that "Bear" was being framed; that the deputy had been killed by a fellow deputy, a "friendly fire" accident, and that his cousin was innocent and wanted to surrender and face the charges if I could represent him. Of course, they were indigent. "Bear" had run only in fear of being killed by law enforcement.

Lawyer Diana Samuelson and I were led
for hours on a riverside trail rising upward in
Mendocino mountains, through forest and thick
foliage. In the remoteness of the area, a Catholic
nunnery was situated, and nearby at an improvised
camping site, we met the "Bear".

His immediate primal force field was
pervasive. He was sturdy, stable, Buddhistic-
like squatting near a stream. He smiled towards
us. His impact was overwhelming, like waves of
charisma emanating from an ancient idol. I knew
then we could never lose the case in court. We had
encountered that rare oddity in death penalty cases,
the 100% innocent defendant.

He repeated his cousin's account of the events.
We agreed to negotiate a surrender for him to our
office in San Francisco. We shook hands and
departed.

Our office was located on and called Pier 5
on the waterfront in San Francisco. It was a three-
storied warehouse converted to
offices. It commanded an encompassing
view of the San Francisco Bay; the Bay Bridge, all

ships and boats that ply those waters. Reflected
sun during the day and reflected moon during the
night spangled and danced into our reconstructed
building. There were over a dozen of us anti-
establishment lawyers fortressed there. It was a hub
of social, political and legal activity.

We surrendered "Bear" in the evening. The
San Francisco Police Captain had promised
safe passage. It was an orchestrated media
event. The alleged "shoot-out" at the Round
Valley Reservation in the mountains of Northern
California, the killing of a white police officer, the
flight and disappearance of the alleged shooter,
the exhaustive futile manhunt for him by police
agencies had made the case one of national interest
to the Native American subculture of the U.S.
Walls of TV cameras lined my office; there were
hundreds of onlookers swelled into the spacious old
warehouse first floor of the "Pier 5 Law Offices".
When Bear appeared, flash bulbs exploded and
handheld microphones extended. Indian leaders
and spokespersons attended. Speeches concerning
Indian rights were made; drums beat; ritual

smoking occurred, and prayers in the native tongues were offered. It was multi-layered. It was a configuration of cultural elements: a death penalty case, an Indian fugitive praised and supported by the Indian community surrendering to law enforcement through the radical lawyer's protective shield; white man's media, police uniforms, Indian children chants and music, flashing camera bulbs-all embraced by the light striking lit gurgling waters of the San Francisco Bay. The police cuffed him, took him out the backdoor. A great silence enveloped all of us remaining. The case had begun. Golden opalescent feathers rained down upon us from the heavens.

This was a national "Indian cause" case. We built a "movement" around it. It had coalesced a social strata. It became a radical, liberal, and an Indian litigation symbol. The potent buzz words of racism and genocide reared its connotations in the defense camp press releases. We possessed an energetic, devoted team that directed and created the political dimensions of the case.

Several Indian bands toured Northern California; fund-raising events were promoted. Speeches, song and dance, drumming, barbecues, press conferences, all glowing and sparkling, enlightened the Mendocino communities, established the political motives of the case in the mentality of the populace. Bear was not a "cop killer"; Bear, like so many Indians before him, was a scapegoat, a martyr to white man's racism. This was a case of police "cover up". "Free Bear" became the call from the mountains of California.

Money from tribes poured in. Prestigious Native American personages appeared at fund-raising activities: eloquent speeches, sweat lodge incantations; reservation to reservation the case flamed into wildfire in the Indian world. Publicity spilled over into the white man's world. When the trial started, Ukiah was invaded by hundreds of supporters: old, young, white, Indian, radical and conservative, circled the small downtown Ukiah courthouse.

Indian music played, dancing, drumming, ritual smoking, food freely disbursed: all on the front lawns of the courthouse. We, in court, were surrounded by the sounds and smells, the chants and songs, the aura and vibration of a teeming public display of support for the "Bear". How could we lose?

As occurred at the surrender of Bear at my office amidst a press conference, and the ritualistic support of the Native American tribes at the outset of trial, the skies opened and hailed upon us on the front lawns of the courthouse a plethora of golden, sun fringed, floating, descending feathers. The reflected yellow luminosity was blinding. We were bathed in scintillating gilt. We were annointed for courtroom battle by flickering rays of light. We were feather kissed by the sun. The Native Americans had opened the vault to heaven and heaven's richness enveloped us.

Usually I was the gold maker, the alchemist who turned the common base metals of facts, of evidence, of thoughts and deeds to gold, to tints and tinctures of gold dust, or golden statues or golden jewelry. I had the magic Midas touch. I was the lawyer magician, alchemist Lord Supreme

of the emblazoned order. Court crowds waited
for my transmutations of the evidence. I was
the Rumpelstiltskin having my witnesses weave
gold from straw. But in the Bear Lincoln case,
the opposite was true. I was the recipient of the
showers of gold, not the provider.

I felt the heat, the glow, the gloss, the bloom
of fervent yellowness. I became part of the corn
harvest, heavy ripe yellow corn protruded from
my extremities. I was a giant sunflower bursting
my blossom in the judicial realm. I was a swarm
of golden yellow bees; I was a thousand canaries
screeching; I was a thousand ripe pumpkins piled in
front of the judge; I was yellow plum and a yellow
sponge; I was yolk and butter. The Indians with
the glory of their faith had reified me thusly. We
were invincible. We could not lose. I was a vortex
around which the gold was spun.

Each morning before court started, a few of
us, the lawyers, would enter the "holding tank",
the cell next to the courtroom where incarcerated
defendants await court to commence. We entered
with an Indian medicine man. Only Bear was

contained in the cell; the medicine man brought
abalone shell and holy bark and herb to be lit.
The smoke circled thick and odorous from the
shell containing the mixture when it was lit. The
medicine man chanted; the smoke enveloped us.
Our minds merged, floated and unified in the fumes.
We entered the court, smoke steaming from our
persons, our clothes, our halos. The courtroom was
perfumed by the odor. The jury entered: they saw,
they smelled, they sensed our unitary force, our
thrust, our religiosity. We were smoked holy men;
not murderers, not mouth pieces; this was not a
trial. This was a religious experience.

The medicine man approached the counsel
table after the jury was seated. He unfurled a
doeskin wrapping on the table top. Bits of bark,
herb, stone, feather and shell were displayed. As
a Christian can hold a bible; as a Muslim can
hold a Koran, so can an Indian, under our First
Amendment, have his holy objects close at hand, at
trial, as his spiritual resource, as his manifestation
of holiness and personal integrity. We performed
the smoking ritual and the unfolding of the holy

objects every single morning of trial, all in full view of the jury. We cast a spell upon them. How could we lose?

Our legal team was extraordinary. Most of our paralegals were Native Americans; I physically resemble Indian features; Omar, a young lawyer in our office who assisted me along with others, also appears Indian. All of us sat beside and behind Bear Lincoln in the courtroom. We enveloped him in our shield of Indian mysticism. Most of our witnesses were Native Americans: the percipient eye-witnesses, the expert witnesses who testified on the historical, political, social and economic factors of Indian existence in Northern California.

I recall the qualification dialogue of the experts. It started almost like a chant: "State your name", "Long Eyes Campfire"; "State your education", "Harvard Ph.D."; "State your expertise", "History of Native American Genocide"; "State your tribe", "Apache". Proud, solemn, straightforward in word and spirit were our Indian witnesses. The courthouse in Ukiah was encircled by Indians; the courtroom was encircled by Indians;

the jurors were encircled by Indians: a circle of truth, a circle of trust, an honest forthright embrace.

Years ago we had utilized the so-called "cultural defense" in the Patrick Hooty Croy case. We were once again employing such inviolable theme. To explain why Bear had fled; why an innocent Indian suspect would flee the police, we embarked on the long historical encounter between the whites: the 49'ers, the frontiersmen, the Army, the vigilantes, and ultimately, the white culture's law enforcement. We re-enacted by map, by statistic, by graphic handed-down verbal accounts the brutal genocide of the local Indian tribes. The river that runs into the Round Valley Reservation, the scene of this case, had in past times run red with Indian blood. The repeated massacres of the Native Americans in the Pacific Northwest, the infamies and brutalities perpetrated upon them brought tears to the eyes of the jurors and all of this heart-rending testimony from the mouths of Indian witnesses flooded the courtroom with pathos and softened the jury to compassion. Many times after an Indian expert had testified, the courtroom, like a church, stood in stately silence and all minds drifted to higher spheres.

Through the trial, Bear, the defendant, sat solid, stoic, Buddhistic, pulsating perseverance and endurance. He represented the entire Indian population that had always resisted by endurance the uneven assault by white culture. He was our golden Indian idol, and we, the lawyers and paralegals, were his fiery, flaming semantic arrows emanating from him in all directions, claiming for him a sanctuary from false charges.

The trial took about two months; all relevant facts were adduced. Round Valley Reservation became a vivid reality for the jurors: the largest mountain valley in California, idyllic at one dimension: fields of oats and hay nestled amidst surrounding peaks, river-fed: horse and cow, fishing and hunting; Indians and whites living in simplistic splendor: small wooden houses, wood burning stoves, children running and playing, feeding on fresh salmon, deer meat and acorn: a few stores, a few bars, a post office and a gas station.

Police from various law enforcement agencies had invaded the valley that day searching for a suspect in an earlier homicide. When a crime was committed on the Reservation, law enforcement became an uncontrolled posse of cowboy and Indian platitudes and ruthlessly handled their so-called investigation. That day, the symbols of law and order were wildly lawless. Every resident's rights were violated: house to house searches, Indians lined up and searched and interrogated; false detentions, no arrest or search warrants; law enforcement on a rampage, guns drawn; Indians manhandled, women and children intimidated and brutalized. A powerful civil rights action would later be brought by a San Francisco civil rights lawyer for the wholesale abandonment of the constitution by the police that day. The travesties under color of law perpetrated on the Indian population that day were an ugly re-surfacing of late 1800 scenarios in the hey day of Indian genocide tactics.

The jury heard Bear himself in his poignant, clear and direct manner of speech, in his simple truth telling of few words, how he and his friend, Acorn, rifle in hand, were seeking to leave Round Valley because of all the police harassment, by an eastern trail over a foothill at the edge of the Valley; how two officers hiding themselves and their vehicle off road opened fire on Acorn, killing him instantly. "For no reason, for no reason." Bear kept exclaiming to the jury. Bear, seeing Acorn dead, ran. The officers fired at him as he ran; he stopped, shot once, and dived off the ledge of the trail into the brush and trees and ran for his life back to the Reservation.

One officer, in his frenzy, while firing fell off the ledge with his automatic weapon still engaged. An errant shot killed his police companion. He wrote in his report that Acorn had fired the first shot, causing the return of fire. Acorn lay dead over his rifle. Ballistics showed that it had never been fired.

The police version of the events was a lie. The jury verdict was a triumphant "not guilty". Indian support, prayers, chants, drums, sweats, and smokes had been rewarded. The jury system had provided justice to a Native American cause. There was a small symbolic peace between the red and the white man, and a small restoration of trust in white man's law established. Bear was released. His team was ecstatic. Celebration serenaded the night. A death penalty case of an Indian allegedly killing a white cop had been defeated.

The meaning, the value, the worth of the case in retrospect, was manifold. It showed that Indian unity produces Indian success. It showed that in the court system, Indians must share in the defense of Indians; it showed that the jury justice system could work for the Native American; it showed that gold begets gold.

I betook myself to a high meadow above Ukiah, above the vineyards, above the lakes, where hawks circle and the deer still graze. The erect dry grasses were bright yellow. The mid-day sun bulged low above me. I lay down in the voluptuous stretching yearning stalks of yellow hay-like growth. I became radiated; a glowing sulphurous ember of vibrating life. I entered and merged with the oneness of the purity of gold. I transmuted; I transcended; I became the disembodied bliss of

summer fruition. We had won; we had prevailed;
we had cast our yellow seeds of light into a dark
domain. My yellowness was content.

The Purple Years

~

The florid colors of the flourishing summer of my life, the radiance of the fires of the sun that had cast me in a golden yellow purity, the harvest time of my career's gold rush, like much zenith in nature, passed imperturbably through rainbow transitions. My yellowhood flamed orange, then to red hot coals providing a blistering heat to my existence. I emoted fire; I burned fierce redness; I entered a short stage of life devoted to my self-consummation. I had traveled from green innocence to yellow maturity to a fiery conflagration at my summit. I became my own idol! I was a red Buddha; I was an arrowhead of fire; I was a scorch and a branding iron; I churned like a bubbling ravine of molten lava. I was arrogant, aloof, imperious; I was a burning splinter in the psyche of the establishment.

My red period was orgiastic. I found my consummate love of female - a red blood kin, purveyor of words like myself - an English language teacher, a molder of minds, a medium of prose and poetry. Together we sang out our spirits and smelted into a unity of red glowing embers. My very finite period of redness was a devotion to the interpersonal, not truly a service to the quixotic mission of my law life.

Then came the sky purple of sundown. Between the redness of the apex and the dark blue of death lies the purple realm of existence. Odors of lilac and lavender, purple wine and purple figs; the jewelry of amethyst, and the ornate velvet Bishop=s purple robe-all adorned my presence. The fresh winds of a magenta sunset, the cooling rains from a purplish sky bathed me, sustained me as I entered my final stage of legal foray. As I became the purpleness of the Bishop, of the Cardinal in the domain of law and courtroom - as I became the wetness of burgundy rain, I realized, we all realized, that I was heading for the Darkness. But for a decade, I would splendor in my stature - the deep, rich, scarlet, crimson symbol of authority - even though an authority image of the anti-thesis.

In my purple robes, I traversed to the Land of Oz, to do battle in a dimension of false gods. I did a jury trial in the Emerald City of Las Vegas. It was a case of gambling casino royalty versus the Black Knight of Montana. I represented the Black Knight.

The case involved the death of casino magnate, Ted Binion, a second generation Las Vegas multi-millionaire of family inherited wealth: famous, controversial, a drinker, a bon vivant, an old leech with a penchant for young easy women, and an incurable heroin addict. At the time of his demise, he is living with a young alleged stripper; he has been banned from his casino because of his addiction, and he is falling deeply into the throes of self-induced degeneration. The stripper has lived common-law with him for more than a year, but no longer can Binion activate any interest in her; his life is a devotion to the Achasing of the Dragon@ - the smoking of heroin; he has become his own worst dragon hallucination.

The night before his death, he buys twelve balloons of Mexican black tar heroin, a potent strain of the drug.

The local coroner concludes his death is by drug overdose. Only a few empty balloons are found on the premises.

Binion had buried in an underground vault, about six million dollars in silver at a secret desert-like location. My client, Rick Tabish, hours after the death of Binion, was arrested at the vault site, having in his trucks the loot. It becomes ascertained that Rick and the stripper were having a clandestine affair, under the guise of Rick's ostensible friendship with and employment by Binion. Under the terms of his will, the stripper will take millions. Binion=s extended family and his ex-wife and child are all outraged. They believe that Rick and the stripper killed their provider to get at his fortune by inheritance and by theft of the silver. They want vengeance.

Rick is an outsider, an owner of a large trucking company, from Montana. The casino insiders see him as a swashbuckling, woman-

stealing, co-murdering thief. Casino royalty wants
the heads of him and the stripper. They will pay
any price for their scapegoat justice.

They hire an ex-Las Vegas police inspector;
he searches the country for a pathologist to say the
death was criminally induced. $80,000 or more
is paid to a media quack from New York City.
He claims Binion was burked, i.e., sat upon and
smothered. After about six to eight months post-
mortem, the local law enforcement are persuaded to
file murder charges against the two lovers. A first
trial ends in their conviction. They are sentenced
to life imprisonment. The Nevada Supreme Court
reverses their convictions. An old radical lawyer
from San Francisco is brought in to defend Rick
Tabish in the re-trial. His name is J. Tony Serra.
He has purple skin. The case becomes a Las
Vegas/Hollywood sensation. Several books have
been written on the sordid details; the retrial will
be a media sharkfest. The Las Vegas populace
has long been inebriated by celebrity images and
sensationalism. The casino/owner royalty reign
supreme in the Vegas world. They have reified from

the barren desert a glittering, tourist-gambling hotel metropolitan society. They live on the cactus fruits of the gambling, the prostitution and the drugs, but have created a strict and severe law and order motif for the general working and visiting population. They live on anomaly and hypocrisy.

Into this quagmire of fact and fiction, I strode in my purple vestments, haughty and oblivious to the dominating claims of the fiefdom. Purplishness creates purple waves of energy that vanquish lesser forces. From the inception of the case, my momentum roared at the Casino Dragon.

I saw the case in simplistic, juvenile metaphors. Rick Tabish-strong, handsome, intelligent; the black knight rescuing the fair damsel from the smoking dragon villain-both of them ensnared by the dragon's allies and held captive in their towers; and I, of violet robe, the purpled wizard, would extricate them. I, master of mauve, to give eulogy for the passing of the demons.

The defense overwhelmed the prosecution. An aged voyeur millionaire funded the stripper's case. We had ample money to bring in the country's leading pathologists. They wholly debunked the wizard of Oz, the state's humbug pathologist. The burking theory of death was resoundly ridiculed. Binion's blood showed enough heroin to have killed an elephant. He had obviously died of drug overdose. The jury took little time to find the pair not guilty of murder.

The crude passion play performed in court had the stereotyped-platitude happy ending. National TV re-echoed the melodrama; talking heads shook their jowls, and the journalists rewrote their books. I went to the mountains outside of Las Vegas, above the high desert; I went alone. They say the mountain gleam with red rock, ancient iron strata streaking angles of blood in the uplifted terrain, but I saw only purple. I swooned mountain high at the purple ridge sawing its way into the purplescent skies. I figuratively cut my wrists, allowing thick purple life fluid to ooze from my spirit and enter into the merger of air and earth. I was in oneness with the purple grandeur. I fell supplicant to the vital live energy of purpleness.

My next two jury trials represented the finest hours of my vintage years of law practice: a return to the idealism of my green period. I helped represent Earth First, an environmental protection group of activists, in their civil rights actions against law enforcement.

The first civil rights case was entitled Judi Bari and Darrel Cherney versus the FBI and the Oakland Police Department. It took about ten years after filing for it to finally be tried to jury. The paperwork had been enormous. Year after year of depositions, motions, interim appeals, lawyer shuffling and financing woes had delayed the trial setting. Judi Bari, the charismatic leader of Earth First, had died of cancer long before the trial started.

Judi and Darrel had been bombed while driving to sing protest songs at an Earth First fund raiser for the Redwood Summer Campaign. The campaign sought legislation to stop the harvest of the ancient redwoods in Northern California. There were street and media antagonisms between Earth First, the environmentalists, the liberals and their adversaries, the lumber interests and their politicians. Strong views on both sides were clashing. Persons and groups as far right as the neo-Nazis had threatened Judi's life several times. Unheeding and fearless, Judi and Darrel, both ballad singers and guitar players, made the sounds for the liberal establishment of Northern California, singing praises to the demonstrators who sought to preserve the redwoods and damning the lumber profiteers who sought redwood tree genocide. Redwood Summer in Northern California was patterned after the voting registration drives in the South during the 50's; youth in the main came from all over the U.S. to Northern California to participate in the Earth First activities promoting the anti-logging legislation, voting registration, demonstrations, parades, musical events, skits, posters, leaflets, singing, chanting, road block lumber trucks, media events, press conferences; all non-violent, burgeoned in the weeks preceding the bomb explosion in Judi's and Darrel's vehicle.

Law enforcement, which had always been perceived to aid the side of the lumber interests, took the bombing as an opportunity to foreclose on the movement against logging. They immediately arrested Darrel and Judi on the pretense that they were themselves the bombers. Each of them were injured by the explosion; Judi seriously. They were police guarded at the hospital and kept incommunicado while the FBI and local law enforcement raided all Earth First offices taking their files and records while the media smeared them and Earth First as being violent environmentalists - the Redwood Summer movement was destroyed; the legislation was never realized.

False affidavits for search warrants for Earth First and affiliate groups were created; false police reports were filed; the First and Fourth Amendments were trampled upon. The opposition voice against lumber capitalism was sought to be squelched.

Meanwhile, prosecutors slowly realized that the case against Darrel and Judi as being the bombers was vacuous. The hole in the vehicle floor was directly under the driver's seat where Judi sat while driving. The bomb ignition required three separate actions: First, a switch had to be turned on. Second, a clock had to be set and time had to pass, and third, there was a motion ignition device - the vehicle would have to be turning or swerving for the explosion to take place. To activate all three of these conditions, Judi and Darrel would have been attempting suicide. It was obvious that the bomb had been planted. No criminal case was ever brought against the two.

After the police raids and the confiscation of Earth First possessions, after the libel and slander against Judi, Darrel and Earth First, after the seeds of destruction were planted to terminate Redwood Summer and the protective legislation, Judi and Darrel were exonerated, but their cause had been defeated and their movement crippled. Thus, the filing of the civil rights action and thus, ten years later, a jury trial in Oakland, California where the explosion had occurred. In all of that ten years, the local police and the FBI had not done one whit of bonafide investigation into the true identity of the bomber, although many leads had been furnished. The trial would involve two hostile forces in fierce legal combat, the Earth First versus the FBI.

There were about six lawyers on our legal team; only two of us were in our purple years. Dennis Cunningham, a civil rights lawyer specialist and I showed purple hair and purple robe throughout. We were the seasoned veterans in the wars against over-zealous and corrupt government. Our purplish aura pervaded the defense table. We cast our prickly, purple, raspberry vines about our opponents in court, entwining and encumbering them. Our scarlet burning torches held high empurpled them. We overpowered police lawyers with our glowing magenta opalescence.

Earth First provided an extraordinary support group to the litigation. Offices were rented in downtown Oakland - a defense media team released press statements each day, organized radio interviews, television appearances and interacted with the established media. Delicious lunches and dinners were prepared for the extended team: organic food, wholesome and tasty prepared and served in a communal style; paralegals arranging for witness interviews, strategy meetings in the evening and on the weekends; demonstrations, musical events and speeches all arranged by the Earth First team. What a privilege, what a pleasure to be a part.

My role was to rely upon my criminal trial experiences of cross-examining arrogant perjurious police officers who had perfected the art of disassemblage. I cast my purpleness upon them. I threw my semantic spears, amethyst pointed at them. I smeared the false faces with purple figs and purple plums. The jury became convinced that they had lied and cheated in their investigation of the bombing. The jury took a view of the bombed vehicle still preserved as evidence. They saw the hole under the driver's seat (not in the foot space of the back seat area as the police claimed). They saw that Judi's injuries went straight up to her butt. They saw the evidence of suspects who hated Judi - who were never interviewed by the police. They saw the political ulterior motives of the FBI. They saw the greed of the lumber owners. They ultimately saw the deceit and falsity of the police, the wrongful arrests of Darrel and Judi, the malicious destruction of the Earth First movement.

The jury found both FBI and Oakland Police
liable for First and Fourth Amendment violations.
They awarded Darrel and Judi $4.2 million as just
compensation. We had won an enormous victory.
We had revealed FBI malfeasance. We all, the
entire extended team, reclined on purple cushions
and smiled in satisfaction. I ate raspberry pie that
night!

The second Earth First case was tried to jury
in San Francisco federal court about two years later.
It also centered around Earth First's attempts to
save the ancient redwoods from being clear-cut by
rapacious lumber interests. The centerpiece image
of the case was young idealists locked arm to arm in
metal pipes surrounding tree stumps in a symbolic
protective manner, being eye swabbed with liquid
pepper spray by police officers holding them
fast and forcing their eyes open to apply the pain
producing swab, so as to force them to unlock their
grasp with the metal pipes. The pitiful screaming
of the mostly young women victims, the barbaric
application of pepper spray swabbed directly on an
opened eyeball, allowed us to label the incident,

"Torture per se". The photographed episode went
around the world via TV. The public was astounded
at this image of police torture of non-violent
American environmentalists. In essence, the civil
rights lawsuit against the police was for their acts
of unmitigated brutality. One girl activist being
manhandled by the police was 16 years old, and on
the video could be heard screaming words to the
effect "Stop it, stop it, we are your children."

Before "locking" on tree stumps, in the
lumber company office, in a congressman's office,
on tractors, on gates; throwing their bodies, so
to speak, between the trees and the saws, each
activist attends a non-violent training session
at a forest camp enclave. They are taught non-
violent resistance, law of trespass, environmental
facts, save the redwoods songs. They prepare to
demonstrate, march, tree sit, and hand lock; media
is invited; it is an essential democratic method
to address emerging reform issues: to spotlight
the inequities to expose corporate greed in their
redwood slaughter. These are idealistic, good young
people: writers, poets, organic food growers, Tai

Chi students, Buddhists, cooks and educators-all non-violent, all dedicated to preserving for future generations the last remaining giant redwoods. And for this devotion to the ultimate health of the planet, they were rudely assaulted by local police aligned with profit-seeking corporations who would sell the redwood to the highest bidder. They were assaulted and tortured. The eye is the most sensitive membrane of the body, the window to the spirit, and these officers desecrated it. The legal team was angry. The lawyers emoted their empathy for the victims. The case looked open and shut for us.

In a civil case in the federal court system, the jury must be unanimous. This case was tried three times to jury. The first two times, it hung; the third time the jury found the police liable but awarded only one dollar damages to the plaintiff. It was a pyrrhic victory for us. The jury had found that the use of pepper spray in the swabbing fashion was excessive force and therefore illegal but that the young, strong, healthy demonstrators had suffered no real injuries, merely a short period of excruciating pain. It was a compromise verdict.

J. Tony Serra

We had stopped the use of pepper spray swabbed
on eye balls of non-violent demonstrators but had
received no compensation for their anguish, and it
had taken three jury trials to gain the police liability
judgment.

We savored in establishing the precedent
ending eye swab of pepper spray but commiserated
greatly that the plaintiffs who had sacrificed
so much at the time and in the pursuing of the
litigation, came away with empty hands.

We learned, with shaking heads, that even in
San Francisco, in the 21st Century, society was for
law and order: that support for police and profit
was more important to the public than the pristine
idealism of moral principles carried by the banners
of their children.

Such was the sorry wisdom of my purple mind.
My purplehood era corresponded to the purple haze
shrouding the nation's vision of its democratic,
egalitarian, honest, fair and compassionate utopia.
Purple represents the grasp for perfection as it
before your very eyes subsides and declines into
the darkness of non-existence. "My country right

or wrong" was the disease infecting the minds of the populace. False patriotism dismantling constitutional based social idealism. We were losing moral vigor in the encroaching purplishness.

A violet hazy mist descended upon me, quenching my regality. I became cast in shadow. I wandered from case to case, court to court, winning, losing, receiving compromised verdicts; sometimes bathed in the slanted rays of a scarlet sunset, sometimes lacerated by purple shafts. Purple pain and purple scars commixed with bars and sparkles of raspberry victories. Ambivalence and self-doubt under purple rain - but attended by the crimson linings, rinds and ridges of ballooned purplescent clouds. I stood singular still in festive wine glowing Bishop's robe. I still reigned as the wizard of the legal podium, a charmed miracle worker, the champion of the vanquished.

From green through yellow, touching red, and now in purple, I had been, and continued to be, a cannabis user, advocate and prophet. I had started by embracing the fabled "green buds" of sativa and had reached my apex in unifying with the mystic states produced by the sacramental use of the "purple haze" of indica: a dark, mysterious full bodied, earthy, aromatic and definitely spiritualized purple bud of the Afghanistan cannabis plant. I remained enshrined, encircled and permeated by a swirl of flower-like fumes of the purple haze. I was centered in this latter phase of my legal career by circles of the rising ether of marijuana smoke. I was haloed holy by it. I waved my sprigs of cannabis buds as a burning lantern, shedding light wherever I traversed.

I defended all type and category of marijuana martyrs: the growers, the manicurers, the distributors, the users, the religious users, the medical users, the recreational users, the young and the old; the rich and the poor. Our common bond was the purple haze. We were brothers and sisters in a planetary movement as deeply felt as religion to establish cannabis as a universally recognized elixir of life; both a sacrament and a medicine, as universal a curative as aspirin, as psychologically enhancing as fine wine, and as esthetically pleasing as a bouquet of roses. We believed our mission to decriminalize cannabis to be righteous, and I proudly bore the logo of the cannabis leaf on my mantle. I was aplomb in purple bud, pomp in the ceremony of the passing of the marijuana pipe. I resided in San Francisco, California; the cathedral, the ivory tower of permissiveness. I was blinded by the shroud of liberty of the situs. I was self-deceived as to the majority of humankind's bias against the smoke of the bud. I was trampled and defeated in many cannabis wars waged in the courtroom battlefield.

One most painfully recalled was a jury trial in Minneapolis, Minnesota, a federal case tried in the snow of winter. The case turned out to be a clash of cultures: the Enlightenment versus the Dark Ages; San Francisco mentality versus the Straight World.

The defendant was a young man, native to San Francisco, handsome and forthright. He had no criminal record, was from a good family, clean cut, with mate and child. He was a marijuana dealer, honest and conscientious. He provided Mexican low-grade product at low, below market prices. He exacted a small commission, a modest profit from his enterprise. He supplied to a desirous and appreciative market. He lived non-materialistically. In San Francisco, California, he was loved and respected by his peer group.

One of his best friends was one of his major buyers. The friend transported the Mexican-grown marijuana to Minneapolis hundreds of pounds at a time. The friend sold it there to a local distributor. These transactions had been occurring for five to six years.

The local Minneapolis distributor was arrested. He quickly turned state informant and set up a police-controlled delivery from my client's friend. The load was about 400 pounds. My client's friend quickly turned informant and set up another delivery from my client. My client was arrested by the DEA in the process of the exchange, caught in flagrante delicti with the marijuana in a back sack about to be transferred.

There really was no defense to the case. My client had been "snitched off" by one of his close friends. He had been caught in the act. The marijuana had been lawfully seized by the police.

The case unfortunately was charged in federal court in Minneapolis, not in San Francisco. We could not get a change of venue.

Minnesotan federal prosecutors were mean-spirited and as cold as the climate. They charged the ill-begotten darling of the prosecution nursery, conspiracy, that ranged over a five-year period. The total weight of marijuana alleged to be involved increased ten-fold. Such was predicated on the word and records of his now informant ex-buddy. He was facing a ten-year minimum mandatory prison sentence, but by guidelines due to the conspiratorial weight quantity, he could get up to seventeen years.

What was, so to speak, de facto legal in San Francisco was sentence butchery in Minneapolis. He had no choice but to go to trial and hope for some form of appellate error. He would have to snitch; he would not plead himself into ten years or more in federal penitentiary. He looked to me, the marijuana champion, the miracle worker, and the purple-robed wizard for justice.

J. Tony Serra

The federal sentencing law is draconian. It is a creature of legislation. Sentencing discretion is taken from the courts in drug cases. The Balance of Powers Doctrine, which is so crucial to our constitutional democracy, has been usurped. The judiciary has been rendered impotent. Sentencing mandated, based on quantity of drugs, must be employed. The war on drugs' greatest victim is the traditional individualized, personal, considered sentence that befits the defendant as well as the crime. With mandatory herculean sentences to fortify their power, the executives, the prosecution, the law enforcement branches of government have become more powerful, more totalitarian than in any previous era of our criminal jurisprudence system.

They, the new KGB, lord over their arrestee prisoners and mentally torture them with the threat of long painful years of incarceration if they do not inform or assist in the arrest of others. Our system of justice becomes informant witness based. Informants, fearful of potentially decades in prison, will say anything to save their own skin.

Informants lie. Everyone who practices criminal law accepts such as a premise of defense. There have been more miscarriages of justice effectuated by informant debriefing, informant exaggeration, informant lies and informant perjury, than any other cause. If a defense lawyer paid for a defense witness to testify, the lawyer would be criminally charged. But the government gives its informants far more precious than money; the government gives liberty, freedom from prison, years and years off sentences, leniency and sometimes no charges at all. The system has become morally bankrupt: torture them to snitch, accept their lies, and reward them exceedingly. The government has congressed all.

Such was our position at trial. The case was essentially my client versus a snitch, plus several hundred pounds of pot. We had no chance. We were buried in purple turf. The jury convicted without hesitation. The defendant received a fourteen-year sentence. He's still appealing! He joins the rank of marijuana outlaws who were martyred in the early 21st century. Marijuana will

be decriminalized. We will look back historically
at these outlaws as folk heroes. The known benefits
of marijuana increase; the national usage increases
each year. The earth is not flat; it is round!
Evolution of humankind toward enlightenment
is a reality. The undue body count of imprisoned
marijuana offenders will be the matrix and humus
out of which understanding, reform and change will
occur.

I tread out of Minneapolis with head bowed,
with the harsh realization of purple death, of defeat,
in darkness, knowing that I had failed my sub-
culture, that I had bestowed no wane glimmer of
hope for marijuana reform in Minnesota - accepting
that the American mainstream was very much pro-
government, pro-police, even pro-informant; that
maybe in my lifetime, we, who served the judicial
branch of a constitutional democracy, had devolved
rather than evolved. Even then, my purple mind
sought readiness for a next confrontation.

Of my cases punctuating my purple period,
three trials figure prominently in my memory that
were venued in Hayward, California. Twice tied

to jury was a case of a transgender of tender age, brutally beaten and strangled, then buried in the foothills of the Sierras. The evidence highlighted the heat of passion reaction of defendants engendered by the sexual deceit of the decedent.

Hayward, California is a San Francisco-Bay Area suburb: a middle-class, working person's community of homesteads situated near the southern reach of the Bay, about forty miles south of San Francisco, cradled between two highways that are major arteries to San Francisco. Essentially, a white and Mexican-American integration, the centerless city consists of housing, unattached, with lawns and detached garages, an image of the American Dream for many working class families: two and three bedrooms, television, two cars in the garage; lives devoted to work, sports, TV, and family raising. The epi-centers being the backyard barbeque and the local tavern.

The flipside of such a social equation is the typical suburban mentality, political innocence, cultural ignorance, a cloistered lifestyle, and among the youth, when not engaged in work ethic labor, the pursuit of the hedonistic pleasures, the life of "partying": booze and drugs, music and promiscuity.

My client, Jason, was the stereotyped product of such an environment: in his early 20's, Mexican-American, first generation, skilled building trade laborer, living with his mother and father, with a pregnant girlfriend living with her parents. He was simple, inarticulate, loyal to friends and family, untraveled, unread - a bundle still of puerile instincts and emotions. A man/boy who never made it past sophomore in high school but who earned union pay and had plenty of money for cars, bars and "partying." Thus also were his male "buddies." Their usual schedule of after work avocations included a Thursday night "party" at one of the defendant's homes-a party defined as booze, pot, speed, music, TV and dominoes, culminating in sexual liaisons with female invitees.

Into this party scene came a beautiful, young neophyte, a feminine fatal, sexually provocative, and a willing drug and alcohol co-mingler. She was somewhat "passed around" by the inner circle of dominant males. She freely bestowed on the pleasure seekers oral and anal sex, always claiming that she was in a menstrual period and prohibiting vaginal intercourse. Months passed of these weekly contacts, and she became suspect of gender category. She was rudely uncovered. Drugged and drunk minds exploded into humiliation and angry rage. "She" became "he"; he was beaten with frying pan; head smashed with heavy can of vegetables, rendered unconscious by kicks and beating, ultimately strangled with a length of rope; the body shrouded in a blanket, thrown into the rear of a truck, driven for six hours distance, and buried in the California mountains.

My client, Jason, a fervent Catholic, in a tearful turmoil, sweared, and would swear on a Bible, that he had not had any form of sex with the young transgender, did not in any way help kill her, but that in a moment of regretful loyalty to his buddies, did go with them to help bury her. He had made bail; he and his parents and brothers and sisters sat around me at my office conference room table. The door was closed; he cried and cried. His mother and father cried. They all swore that he was telling the truth. "Please, please, take my son's case, Mr. Serra."

In green, in yellow, I would have refused. In purple, my heart took pity. In purple, there is a deep empathetic, compassionate emotion that swells scarlet blood like from the well of your inner recesses. It divests you of logic and reason. Jason was the impoverished bud of this family tree that surrounded me. I could not reject their painful plight. Thus I engaged to take a case whose symbolism breached my stature of righteous radical lawyer. I was pledged to swim against my own tide. I was on the wrong side of a gay, lesbian, and transgender movement cause case. I would be seen as protecting counter-evolutionary behavior, promoting the narrow motives of instinctual natural selection, championing primitive, primal response to gender misrepresentation, to be alleging as a defense that the transgender by deceit had sown the seeds of her own fatality, that she had perpetrated the sexual misconduct. That the defendants had merely reacted to her fraud on their young virility.

That she/he had not been murdered; that the defendants had been psychologically provoked by their "heat of passion." That their reason had been clouded and transformed; that their actions were instinctual, not premeditated or deliberated and that they were guilty only of manslaughter.

The case was a media circus. Books, movies and TV documentaries were done on it. It was cause célèbre in the gay lesbian communities. I was carrying the banner of anti-gay resistance. I had betrayed my allies. I was in league with the rednecks!

I was conflicted. The burning purple flame within me illuminated upon the central core criterion for any criminal defense attorney. My client Jason shined with the iridescence of innocence. Here was that rare jewel in criminal jurisprudence: the "innocent man", the wrongfully charged, and the falsely vilified. Should not the purity of the gleaming purplish light that bathed him have the greatest priority? Do I sacrifice his purity for my ego, for my reputation? I could not. I did not.

But our defense would not be the heat of passion defense relying on justifiable behavior in consideration of the sexual deceit provocation. Our defense would be the simple proposition that Jason did not do it. He did not have cause to do it. He did not help do it. He was an accessory after the fact only. He had foolishly helped his friends dispose of the body, but no more than that.

We would not join the other three defendants who were claiming manslaughter. We therefore were not seeking to justify the killing by pretending that the actions bordered on an involuntary psychiatric reaction. We did not have to demean the behavior of the transgender. We were not resisting the ideology of the transgender constituency. Such was our announced concretized position. But the media-like sharks with flesh in their bite would not let us go. Our defense was blurred into unison with the others in the press presentations. It became the greatest litigation of mixed metaphors in my career.

One of Jason's "buddies" turned state's evidence against him to obtain leniency, an 11-year sentence for manslaughter. But even then, Jaron, the snitch, who admitted that if he had gone to trial, he would have been found guilty of first degree murder, and had never testified that he saw Jason do anything violent that night. Further, Jaron admitted that he had a "character flaw" of chronic falsehood. Jason testified. His lack of schooling, lack of self-confidence in language usage, his fears of being convicted by his association with the others, his natural shyness and introversion created an image of hesitancy and incompleteness. He was never caught in a lie, but his inarticulateness and timidity rendered him oblique and vulnerable.

Both times the case was tried, the jury hung for Jason. The second trial ended in murder convictions for the other two defendants. Approximately six months of jury trial was devoted to the case. Jason had done about two years jail time before he got bail. We compromised rather than go a third round. We took a "no contest" plea for six years, to a manslaughter charge. He would have to do about three more years prison time. The media had convicted all four of them. Jason had barely managed to sneak by. The public was

outraged at the bestial response of these young
men to the revelation that their sex object was an
anatomical male. It was deemed not the actions
of a reasonable person in like circumstances. It
was denounced therefore by jury and spectators
as unacceptable behavior in response to sexual
deceit. The victim became a media-created
folkloric heroine. The San Francisco Gay Lesbian
Transgender Community demonstrated and paraded
on her behalf. Television audiences wept for her;
her mother became a champion of the transgender
movement for recognition and understanding of
the transgender challenges. Two of the accused
will spend the rest of their lives in prison for their
primal, "gut" reaction to their humiliation. The
snitch, equally culpable to those two, got away with
eleven years and my client's justice was swept away
in the spillover. But he will be released in three
years and the criminal judicial system will never
hear a peep from him again.

So ended the long tale of travail. In the second
trial I was assisted by a young openly gay lawyer
in our office. His understanding and compassion

for Jason somewhat alleviates my taint in the gay community for being involved in the matter. Once again my purple cloth was cut and sliced, my plush raiments defiled, my purple hair pulled and torn, my purple tears flowed, but I did survive.

As the fading spectral glories dim for the semantic warrior in his purple years, he retreats to his most basic philosophy of engagement with government forces. He exercises only his most fundamental tenets of belief system; he embodies his own ideological rudiments, the longest accepted dogma is lawyer's creed. Win or loss is not the criterion; the exposure and revelation of the flaws, the infamies, the inequities and the transgressions of the opposition become the lights striven for- violet, velvet, purplescent consciousness of the scarlet radical lawyer.

Thus for me in this decade of my meditation upon my own magenta sun-setting, my jury trial caseload to the casual observer could appear random and unselective, without boundary or common thread. I assure you, it was otherwise. I sought purely to fester and aggravate the wounds

and lacerations already observable on the social-
political organism establishment. My verbal darts
and arrows were always aimed at inflaming the
perspectives upon the overwhelming presence
of racism, economic oppression and inequity in
the criminal justice system: to manifest the pain,
agony, fear and rage of the discarded, the rejected,
the scorned of the dominant society. Mine was
the mission to raise specters of discomfort for the
complacent mentality of the sleeping masses by
showing them the photographs taken in jury trials
of the acts and judgments of quiet desperation
that lurked below the surface of their indifference.
Revelation of the pain of aggrieved people is the
first stage of change. Outrage produces reform.
Mine was the angry linguistic fist raised rudely
and mightily in the face of the power of the elite.
My countenance shined with purpled scars of past
conflict. I glared and glowered at the prosecution;
I sought their ideological vulnerabilities and thrust
my purple-poisoned spear into its inners.

The typical, symbolic-laden type case that I
would try to jury in this latter stage of my career

is exemplified by an assassination death jury trial occurring in Alameda County, California. The case was a defenseless stance against a charge of first degree murder leveled upon a high ranking Hispanic gang leader of Nuestra Familia, for allegedly shooting to death one of the gang's lieutenants over an unpaid drug debt.

Nuestra Familia is said to be a strident street and prison gang, organized in para-military style, comprised of Hispanic youth dedicated to their perceived racial infinities and engaged in drug sales and extortions. Their basic motivation, aside from personal status achievement, is to enhance the well being of their entire minority. Their members ranged from street toughs to political theorists. The defendant that I was to represent was of the intellectual component. While his brother was earning a Ph.D. at U.C. Berkeley, he was creating the doctrinal political philosophy that underpinned the Nuestra Familia movement. He was, within his genre, a soft-spoken, intense, articulate, uncompromising zealot - his title gifted upon him by his soldiers was "The Beloved One." He was, in his milieu, in and outside of prison, a walking demi-god.

Thin, angular; piercing, threatening black eyes, tattooed body, "Nuestra Familia" in bold four inch block letters across his chest; he was fearless of police, guard, prison or conviction. His life would be the same, in or out of incarceration. He was one hundred percent the embodiment of his cause.

To sit next to him in court was to be inflated by his terse charisma. Always in voce dolce, he championed our position and supported his defense. He never cowered, never complained, and never regretted his predicament. I became very proud to be his lawyer.

The killing had occurred in a low class trailer park in the doorway of a trailer home occupied by a meth user, small time dealer. The victim had phoned that he was coming by. It was dark. Out of the shadows two men came. One shot him several times point blank. The two assailants then casually walked away. The victim had come with two friends, who remained in the parked vehicle about thirty feet away. The two eyewitness friends were under the influence of meth; were blinded by gun focus, had given to police descriptions of the two, none of which matched my client. Later, after three years, they would change their stories and ID the defendant as the shooter, telling the jury that they had been intimidated previously and therefore fearful to tell the truth. Their new versions conflicted with each other; they had little credibility. The only other evidence was gang paraphernalia, Nuestra Familia bylaws and policy statement, but no gun, no drugs, no confession. But for the star witness snitch, the case would technically be won.

The major witness against us was a lifetime Nuestra Familia member, a sort of lieutenant in gang rank; a street-wise, medium level drug distributor; a man convicted multiple times of felon drug dealing, a felon who had served half of his life in prisons, who now faced another long sentence. He offered himself as an informant to law enforcement, as an insider privy to the secrets and clandestine operations of Nuestra Familia. He was bold; he would testify against "the Beloved". He knew all details of the assassination, allegedly from my client's own mouth. In exchange for his cooperation, he wanted freedom and safe passage out of California. The bargain was made with the District Attorney. He would be the People's star witness. I begged my client to allow me to postpone his trial. In another year, I believed, that this informant would run or recant, and then we might prevail at trial. The eyewitnesses were conflicted and lacked credibility. Our only chance was that the informant might be bluffing to gain his freedom and then disappear. The client told me calmly, "No, don't postpone the trial. He he will never testify."

The informant was in custody. He had been attacked allegedly by Nuestra Familia inmates. His cheek extending down to his neck had been knife slashed. The wound healed and scarred. He testified for days to the intimate details of the gang activities and to the death of the gang victim. He told the jury that Nuestra Familia, like government itself, had its rules and laws, that failing to pay a drug debt after due time allowance and warnings was a death penalty offense. The victim realized such and the "Beloved One" had himself administered the gang justice of execution. I cast as much purple dirt and purple dust on the snitch witness as available, but the gruesome scar corroborated his testimony. The defendant did not testify. The jury convicted him; they feared gangs; they feared him. They saw the informant as the lesser of two evils. Only my client's mother and father cried tears for him. He would be spending the rest of his life in prison. His parents really never understood his path chosen to lead a prison gang. They had emigrated from Mexico; they participated in the American Dream-hard work, home, family, education for their children. They loved their son, but his form of idealism they could not comprehend.

This had been a post-9/11 trial. The suburban jury members were impregnated with great fear and trembling. They were afraid of terrorists; they were afraid of bombs, afraid of drive-by-shootings, afraid of gangs, afraid of drunk drivers. Their emotions had been constantly stirred by the media. The police were their protectors; the prosecutors were their shields. They would have convicted an alleged leader of a violent, drug-dealing gang of being a member of Al Qaeda if it had been charged. Their only concern, the whole case, was that they be protected from potential retaliation from Nuestra Familia.

My client never told me that he did it. I never asked!

Why would I take such a case, such an unwinnable case, such a cold blooded murder case? Was my purple mind muddled? Had I lost my moral compass? No, let me tell you the meaning of it.

First, to voice, identify and dignify the protest of excluded minorities. The dysfunction of the dominant culture had produced the dysfunction of the subordinate culture. This case and all like it are challenges to racism and class struggle. If Hispanics are treated fairly in the job markets, in the access to education, in the law, and in the economy, there would be no need to establish an alternative subculture with its own laws, army and system of law and order. The case screamed out to us to re-think the assigned social economic status of Mexican immigrant families.

Second, Nuestra Familia was established primarily to obtain for Mexican-American youth respect, self-respect and respect from the dominant white culture. Respect is manifest in a society bestowing prominence, education and economic security in its co-occupants. Because there is no respect given by the dominant culture to the Mexican immigrant and offspring, they must establish it themselves by creating a new social political economic order of reality. Because they have not been allowed into the general pyramid of our culture, they must build their own pyramid. The case is a cry from the New Testament - give unto others, what you would have them give unto you!

Lastly, the case was another episode of trial by paid informant. Here, a gang member, drug-dealing felon is given years and years of freedom from prison. He would say anything for such a prize. Informants corrupt the integrity of the judicial system. Snitch leniency erodes the truth seeking process of litigation. The Judas system of justice can never be trusted. Informant testimony is a cancer in the honesty of the process of jury trial. We can never know if a paid informant is telling the truth or lying. The sad thing is that we, as a society, just don't care. The thin blue line of police protection has become our thick blue wall that strangles fairness and incarcerates freedoms. These are the kind of cases where we, the defense lawyers, can make our stand against encroaching Orwellian totalitarianism.

Despite the loss, my purple banners hung highly from the ceiling, from the walls, from the tables and chairs of the courtroom. Truths greater than the truth of conviction had emanated from the forum. The courtroom emptied. I was the lone occupant; the lights were dimmed. A purple radiance permeated the atmosphere. I took off one purple shoe and pounded it loudly on the podium over and over again.

How long does purplehood last? When does purple dissolve to black? When does the mind stop flinting light back on its own thought processes?

At what age does the semantic sword become too weighty to bear? Will I recognize the darkness when it vanquishes my purpleness?

These and myriad more are the long, long thoughts of the aging radical lawyer incarcerated in a federal prison camp, my second sojourn to prison for IRS misdemeanor convictions. For over four decades, I have been a tax resistor. I have been charged and convicted thrice over such period: one time sentenced to probation; two times sentenced to federal prison camp; the first time for four months, the second time, at present, for ten months. Tax protest founded in principle, not greed, is not considered moral turpitude by the State Bar Association, so my legal license has never been revoked.

My mind paces like a tiger in a cage awaiting freedom to resume the struggle, but in the hiatus, I weigh and balance the chromatic metaphors of law practice during the green, yellow and now purple stages of my career.

I am presently a prisoner because I do not pay my taxes. For many years, I did not pay and

did not file. I now file but still resist payment.
Tax boycott started as a popular Vietnam War
protest in my green years; later in my yellowhood,
similar ideology became a causative component
of unwillingness to support the U.S. government.
And presently in the purple years, an attitude of
Buddhistic indifference is a primary factor in my
non-compliance. I recognize tax boycott now is
quixotic. The mentality of the U.S. citizenry is,
for the most part, blind obedience to the fiats of the
empowered class: no protests, no demonstrations,
no resistance, no uproar or rage to any demands
put to it by government or industry. Where are the
Thomas Paines, the Thoreaus and the Emersons?
Why are we a nation of huddled sheep? The U.S.
government is hated and feared by the greater world
population but the U.S. populace remains mute and
subservient stripped of fundamental democracy,
shorn of its basic constitutional rights, wage slaves
to the capitalists. We surrendered our freedoms to
an encroaching totalitarian state, without a whimper.

    I see at prison camp the glazed-eyed stare of
the mandatory sentence martyrs. I embrace the

pathos of the discarded victims of a draconian judicial penal system. I absorb the cruelty, the unfairness of the long incarcerations of youth, of the impoverished, of the uneducated, of the aged. I touch the legions of prisoners walking the prison circles for decades of their lives: no probation, no parole, and no touch of woman; their emotions withered and waned, an outcast society of living dead. We have more prisoners, more prisons, and more forfeited lives to the judicial system, than any other country in the history of the world. These are my brothers; I will not forsake them. My purple warrior-hood will continue after release.

Prison camp is benign. Its heartbeat is UNICOR, prison industries garnering millions of dollars for the Bureau of Prisons, predicated on the slave labor of the inmates. Prison camps exist to furnish involuntary servitude to government sponsored, profit-taking work projects: cattle raising, dairy production, meat distribution, farming, cable factories; all employing the prisoners for pennies per hour. But the camp itself masks the ugly exploitation. Green lawns, plants, swaying eucalyptus trees, gardens, sleeping barracks, library, chapel-all anesthetize public awareness of the existence of these modern day correlatives to the Siberian exile work camps of Stalin.

I am a camp waterman - I'm a "rainmaker", a "river"; I am called the "Rainbow Man" by the inmates. I revel in the esthetics of the environment, but I maintain a steel hard perspective on the basic inhumanity of the prison conditions.

For a purple man, the camp tenure affords ample time for existential self-study, the freedom to pursue esthetic and pantheistic thought, to engage intellect with reading, writing, and poetry. The emancipation from the self-willed discipline of delineated focus on legal issues, the activation of passive vocabulary to articulate notions of love and beauty - to further the ongoing quest for life's meaning. But such self-development becomes ultimately selfish and circumscribed.

The true calling of the incarcerated condition is the patient preparation for the return, for the sojourn's merger with its departure, for the resumption of battle. It is a rest and a reward given on the basis that the return to the battlefield will be resurrected, revitalized and more resolved. So it is for purple pride and purple plan and purple mission still intact.

But in these interim months, prison camp is my sanctuary. I wear the dark empurpled robe of the monk. My eyes glint purplish fire. I am the Cardinal of the judicial system incarcerated. I am the Bishop of law in penance; I am the Priest of logos ensnared in his own logic. I perform the holy rites of the legal profession. I am a lawyer in prison still licensed to practice. I hold my purple ambered torch aloft for all prisoners to bathe within.

With solemn bowed head and averted eyes on wooden bench amidst flower, plant and tree, I hear the confessionals of the inmates. They murmur low their confidential communications. I absolve them all!

They stripped me naked of my constitutional rights. They said I was a terrorist. They tapped my phones, sold me stolen merchandise; they set me up. I am innocent. I am not a terrorist. I believed in the American Dream. They are racist; the government doesn't care. I am here because I am Muslim. I didn't know the products had been stolen. My family is destroyed.

I nod my agreement with his scenario. I tell him to persevere. We discuss his appeal. I instill optimism upon his despair. The calling of the purple warrior in penal penance is to receive confidences, to counsel, to advise and to support the psychological stability of the inmate, planting hope and meaning in their pain and frustration.

A white collar businessman, stern and serene, tells me,

It was only a loan from my own corporation. I would have given it back. It shouldn't have been made a crime. It was a pure civil matter. I should never have been charged. This country is going to the dogs. If I was out, I would be employing hundreds of workers and paying tax. Why put me in jail? It is hurting the economy. I did not harm anyone. At most, it should have been a fine.

So goes the anti-government incantation. I nod my head in agreement. We collectively disparage the federal government.

The younger inmates, whose youth has been taken by the harsh sentencing, the mandatory minimums of the sentencing guidelines, render to me their voices of despair:

It was only marijuana. I thought marijuana wasn't treated so harshly by law. I wasn't selling it very long. I wasn't making much profit. I was just having a good time. I'm only 22. They gave me 14 years.

Or another:

In California, if you get a doctor's letter, you can grow marijuana legally. I thought it was okay. I thought the feds would leave me alone. I'm in prison for doing something I thought was legal.

I nod my head in agreement. I tell them that feds have power and want more power. That they have no compassion, that their investigations and charges and the court sentences are unjust. That the inmate is morally right and the government morally wrong. That the U.S. is becoming a police state.

We sit, we talk, and we commiserate. I talk intimately with drug makers, the drug seller, and the drug mule. I talk with the smuggler, the street dealer and the users. I talk with corporate heads, men of position and prestige. I talk to all level of inmates, all races and convicted of all manner of crime. They cry out in united voices that they have been treated unfairly by the justice system. They tell me, "Tony, you can do something about it when you get out. Tell them how it is. Don't forget us."

I nod my head in agreement. The most common complaint of the inmate was the ineffectual legal representation that they received:

The lawyer never visited me. He never prepared the case. He didn't file any motions. I didn't hear my side of the story. I said I would lose. I would do greater prison time. He told me to sign the plea agreement. It was right before trial date. He had not even read the whole file. What could I do? I signed away all my rights. I never had a trial.

He sold me out. He did not care. I was forced to plea.

So went the countless, soft soliloquies on my lawyer's bench in the garden of the prison camp. In the quiet blur of purple minds merging, I administered my sacred oath of empathy for prisoner and respect for his plight. I applied my verbal balm. I joined in the distress and the disdain of the inmate for law enforcement.

Now was my quiet time: no clash of courtroom rhetoric, no win-loss symbolism, no enraptured jury, no drama, no celebrations for victory or bewilderment for loss. This was my interlude of service to the downtrodden by reading and writing, by listening, by comforting, by advice and opinion. My office was the outdoor benches, the library and the bunk side folding chairs. Much suffering, much protest and many challenges were received in these locations.

I knew little of the criminal law specialty of post-conviction remedies, the possible writs, the civil actions, the prison administrative process that ripens an issue for the courts. I listened to prisoner complaints about work assignments, pay, visiting, phone calls, illness, searches, punishments and harassment. A Christian who was disallowed to change his faith to Muslim, an inmate put in the hole for writing to the administration for change of diet, an inmate punished for falling asleep in the chapel and missing count, an inmate whose foot infection eventuated into amputation of part of his toe, an inmate not discharged in time, an inmate denied halfway house, an inmate whose commissary money had been partially seized for restitution, an inmate whose legal mail had been opened by the guards, an inmate whose wristwatch had been confiscated for wearing it to visiting, an inmate whose telephone privilege had been suspended for inappropriate language on line: the list went on and on. I provided mostly solace, nothing really remedial or reformative, but a willing ear, and understanding and compassionate response.

I learned to help write the writs, the habeas corpus last hopes. I came to recognize the righteous issues and the legal vehicles by which to broadcast them. I could eventually talk the talk of the jailhouse lawyer - using euphemisms of the trade: "2241", "2255", "1983", "Petition", "Traverse" and "Reply". I explained some of the esoteric verbiage, the meaning of such pronouncements as "res "judicata", "affirmed", "remanded", "with prejudice", "without prejudice", "writ of error corum nobis", "indigent", "en banc" and "standing".

To counsel, to edify, and to assist the inmates in extricating themselves from the cobweb of legalese was my succor and satisfaction, an appropriate function of my purple period. I assisted one prisoner with his writ protesting the search that led to his arrest; I assisted another in correcting a long sentence invalid under sentencing law newly announced by the U.S. Supreme Court; another whose gun possession enhancement was contrary to the law on the subject. I helped many by showing the ways that their lawyers had been ineffectual and incompetent, or had failed to bring meaningful motions, or had failed to object to illegal and damaging evidence.

J. Tony Serra

I revisited law school knowledge in matters
that were civil rather than criminal law. Prison torts
that resulted in pain and injury to an inmate, being
gored by a bull on the farm; inadequate medical
response to illness or accident; forfeiture issues,
civil rights actions, restitution orders, still pending
criminal and civil litigations. I did divorces and
traffic tickets for the prisoners.

In short, I re-established my legal domain
from adversarial combat in courts of law to aider
and abettor of prisoners' grievances and search
for redress. No gallery of court watchers, no
articles the next day in the newspapers. No one
sees the non-spectacular actions of the library
counselor, of the letter writer of the habeas corpus
writ protagonist, but such is the unseen brick and
mortar of prison reform and penal justice. It's an
old man's work; it befits the purple years. It's the
last battlefield against the overreaching tentacles of
government abuse.

The Aftermath

~

It has been a few years since release from prison camp and the writing of this book. I'm close to 80 years old now. The only change in my lifestyle is that I go to bed earlier and get up earlier than before. My ideology and my pursuit of it remains constant. I'm still tilting at Quixotic windmills. I still find rapture in my role as an angry semantic fist. Body weary, mind strong, obsessive determination to challenge the precepts of the establishment, fearing neither loss or death - an aberrant idealist, a raven amongst crows.

Since released from Federal Prison, I have undertaken a frenzy of criminal jury trials to maintain my semantic warrior status and my self-perceived role of exposing the inadequacies of the system. I haven't slowed down. I have increased the pace.

J. Tony Serra

I have taken cases all over the country: Arizona, Washington, Montana, South Dakota, Kansas, New Jersey, Texas, North Carolina and Florida. I have traveled to almost every county in Northern California. I am trying cases in both state and federal jurisdictions. I am a workaholic now and proud of it.

But ever as darkness envelopes my forensic stage, I proclaim proudly that I am the best pro bono lawyer in the court houses. I crave death during a final summation. The jury will cheer "Not Guilty" over my excelsior flag embedded in the podium.